W9-BXX-200

Alcyone

SUNY Series in
Contemporary Continental Philosophy

Dennis J. Schmidt, Editor

Alcyone

Nietzsche on Gifts, Noise, and Women

Gary Shapiro

STATE UNIVERSITY OF NEW YORK PRESS

Published by
State University of New York Press, Albany

© 1991   State University of New York

All rights reserved

Printed in the United States of America

No part of this book may be used or reproduced
in any manner whatsoever without written permission
except in the case of brief quotations embodied in
critical articles and reviews.

For information, address State University of New York
Press, State University Plaza, Albany, N.Y. 12246

Production by Ruth East
Marketing by Bernadette LaManna

Library of Congress Cataloging-in-Publication Data

Shapiro, Gary, 1941–
    Alcyone : Nietzsche on gifts, noise, and women / Gary Shapiro.
        p.   cm. — (SUNY series in contemporary continental
    philosophy)
    Includes bibliographical references and index.
    ISBN 0–7914–0741–1. — ISBN 0–7914–0742–X (pbk.)
    1. Nietzsche, Friedrich Wilhelm, 1844–1900. Also sprach
Zarathustra. 2. Gifts. 3. Noise. 4. Women. I. Title.
II. Series.
B3313.A44S43   1991
193—dc20
                                                    90–48444
                                                        CIP

10 9 8 7 6 5 4 3 2 1

For Marya, David, and Rachel

CONTENTS

GENEALOGY

This book would not have been written but for Walter Brogan's kind invitation to teach a week's course on *Thus Spoke Zarathustra* at the Collegium Phenomenologicum in Perugia, in 1988. At that time I had completed *Nietzschean Narratives* and thought that I would move on to other concerns. But as Nietzsche once wrote to Georg Brandes, "Once you discovered me, it was no great feat to find me: the difficulty now is to lose me." So I found myself that summer developing thoughts that had remained in the background of that first book, thoughts that perhaps constituted something like a photographic negative in relation to its black and white image. For discussion and encouragement in that remarkable Nietzsche summer at Perugia, I am indebted to many students and faculty, but especially to Walter Brogan, Dennis Schmidt, Charles Scott and Hugh Silverman. I'm grateful to Walter Brogan and David Farrell Krell for careful readings of the manuscript and to Dennis Schmidt for urging me to publish the work in the series where it now appears. Elisabeth Caron first alerted me to the importance of the work of Michel Serres and provided a sensitive reading of the first draft of Chapter 3.

For a good start on my Italian journey I am indebted to a fellow American passenger on the first leg of my flight, whose name I have (perhaps significantly) forgotten. We struck up a conversation and I discovered that he was a physician, while he seemed pleased to learn that I was a philosopher (or "philosophist" as he preferred to say). Although he was quite curious to know what we "philosophists" did, he was emphatic in expressing his distaste for those who expected him to give free medical advice. So it was with some trepidation and only after lengthy preliminaries that I dared to ask him for suggestions on how to deal with the jetlag that I was facing. His answer was that there was a drug perfectly suited for the purpose and he offered me samples on the spot. "Would you like some halcion pills?" he asked. I had not yet heard of this remarkable *pharmakon*, which does indeed do what the physician promised (and perhaps more). It certainly proved to have a dormitive virtue and so eased me insensibly into Italian and Nietzschean time. When I asked my seatmate the significance of the pill's name he suggested that it meant "sleep": readers of this book's last chapter will be able to reconstruct the stages by which Alcyone's name has been inscribed in the contemporary pharmacopeia. It was only after I related this story some days later that Dennis Schmidt informed me that *halcion* is suspected of causing memory losses (perhaps it aids in the forgetting of metaphysics). In any case I understand that this modern version of *nepenthe*, which technologizes Nietzsche's *aktive Vergesslichkeit* at least for a night at a time, is now banned in Boston.

    Among my other debts are these: to Janice Doores for patient and careful word processing, to my colleagues in the Department of Philosophy and the Graduate School of the University of Kansas for their support of this project, including an international travel grant that allowed me to teach at Perugia, and to Chris Sharp for her help in preparing the index.

CITATIONS

Citations of Nietzsche's works in the text are generally in this form: (*EH*, 219; *6*, 259). The first reference is to an English translation, the second to the *Kritische Studienausgabe*, edited by Giorgio Colli and Mazzino Montinari (Berlin: Walter de Gruyter, 1980). The first number refers either to a page number or a numbered section of the text; numbered sections in the case of *The Birth of Tragedy, Beyond Good and Evil, The Case of Wagner,* and *Toward a Genealogy of Morals,* page numbers in the case of *Ecce Homo* and *Thus Spoke Zarathustra.* References to letters are to pages of the following edition.

Abbreviations and Translations

B   Friedrich Nietzsche, *Briefe,* 8 volumes, Giorgio Colli and Mazzino Montinari (Berlin, 1986).

BGE   *Beyond Good and Evil,* translated by Walter Kaufmann (New York, 1966)

BT   *The Birth of Tragedy and The Case of Wagner,* trans. Walter Kaufmann (New York, 1967)

CW   *The Case of Wagner,* trans. Walter Kaufmann (with *BT*), (New York, 1967)

EH   *Ecce Homo,* trans. Walter Kaufmann (with *GM*) (New York, 1968)

GM   *On the Genealogy of Morals,* trans.Walter Kaufmann
     (with *EH*), (New York, 1968)

GS   *The Gay Science,* trans.Walter Kaufmann (New York,
     1974)

WP   *The Will to Power,* trans.Walter Kaufmann and R. J.
     Hollingdale (New York, 1968)

Z   *Thus Spoke Zarathustra,* trans. R. J. Hollingdale
     (New York, 1961)

Prelude: Nietzsche and Archaic Economies

Taking my cue from Socrates, in the *Phaedrus*, I might describe this attempt at reading Nietzsche's *Zarathustra* and some of its associated texts as a palinode. After showing that he can compose a better speech of seduction in behalf of the nonlover than Lysias can, Socrates recants and delivers his palinode, a magnificent speech in behalf of the lover that contains the great myth of the soul's sprouting of wings. It will be seen that my palinode (really an attempt to *hear* some of Nietzsche's songs) also invokes a certain flutter of wings as well as some other figures of the Nietzschean animal world. In an earlier study, *Nietzschean Narratives*, I tried to show that Nietzsche the storyteller had been neglected in favor of Nietzsche the aphorist and fragmentary thinker. It was incumbent upon me, then, to show that at least some of Nietzsche's texts could be read either as structured narratives or as engaging at a deep level with the nature of narrative discourse. While not retracting all of those readings, I believe that there are other keys and tones in Nietzsche's musical repertoire worth listening to. Nietzsche, especially in his last writings, always is asking his readers to hear him aright, with the proper ear, and with a sense for his tone; and as with any piece of complex and difficult music what one hears develops and changes with repeated listenings. And whatever excessive degree of bravura might be found in Nietzsche's claim to be the master of more styles than any other writer, his compositions surely cannot be reduced to program music. What follows, then, is at least a song sung in another tone than the earlier one. Nietzsche, of course, was no stranger to such musical battles, as he demonstrates toward

1

the end of *Zarathustra*, whose orchestration is discussed in "Parasites and Their Noise." At the same time it should be obvious that every reading of Nietzsche is a performance as well as an act of observation. If Nietzsche's books are gifts they do not determine once and for all what their recipients will do with them.

The topics announced here—gifts, noise, and women—are hardly central to the philosophical canon as usually conceived, and so it should be evident that I have little interest in reclaiming Nietzsche for such a canon. However, it is worth recalling at a time when canons and the canonization of texts, syllabi and curricula of all sorts are in question, that one of the prominent senses of *canon* is that of a musical order or discipline. I mean to ask in part just how we might hear Nietzsche but also how listening to him might sensitize our ears to other tunes and even to the noise or static against which philosophers take such great precautions and which sometimes is given the ambivalent name of empiricism. Gifts, noise, women: of these only one, women, is likely to be recognized as having been addressed by a number of major thinkers and most will take that to be at best an unfortunate lapse and at worst a reason for rejecting the thinkers and their work wholesale. Nietzsche, because he is so often taken to be a philosopher of culture, risks being tested by his supposedly misogynistic "views" on this subject to an extraordinary degree. I want to suggest that, beyond any such views, maxims, declarations, or anecdotes, we would do well to hear a certain tone, the one that Nietzsche calls *halcyon*, that resounds here and there throughout his texts.

The topics (*topoi* or places) that I have attempted to articulate here perhaps could be given a sort of perverse legitimation by seeing them as the antitheses or anticoncepts of certain notions that have a more obvious philosophical currency. Consider the gift, which seems to be a deviant form or special case of the notion of property. Any social or political philosophy must deal with the question of property. There is a casuistry of property that considers whether ownership ought to be based on inheritance or labor; what limits should there be on one's use of one's private property; and what rights may the state have to tax and regulate property. At a more general level the question arises of whether property ought to be vested in the individual or the state. What are gifts in such a perspective? They are gratuitous, anomalous, and superfluous; that these very terms should have become so close in their meanings indicates the double need both to marginalize these unusual economic activities and to recognize them in their peripheral and exceptional status. Anthropologists like Marcel Mauss have suggested that in what we call archaic economies the gift is primary and what we call property (whether belonging to the individual or the state) is a category not easy to recognize. The archaic is both the ancient and primitive as well as the principle or primary thing; following this suggestion we might ask whether modern exchange and ownership are secondary and derivative practices. If the gift is the uncanny *other* of property, we may well ask whether these thoughts and social practices have deeper metaphysical roots and affiliations. For something to be my property is for me to own it, that is, for it to be a part of my extended self or larger identity. Hegel is quite clear on this:

> By the judgment of possession, at first in the outward appropriation, the thing acquires the predicate of "mine." But this predicate, on its own account merely "practical" has here the signification that I import my personal will into the thing. As so characterized, possession is *property*, which as possession is a *means*, but as existence of the personality is an *end*. In his property the person is brought into union with himself.[1]

Writing at what he takes to be the end of metaphysics, Hegel makes explicit the connection in Western thought between personality and property. Of course this is not the end of Hegel's account, for he immediately adds that property implies recognition by others and so refers us to a community, each member of which is an actual or potential owner of property. The thought can be developed in various ways. Max Stirner, in *Der Einzige und sein Eigentum* (*The Individual and His Own*) took it in an anarchist direction, whereas Karl Marx attempted to rethink property in terms of human species being. Anthropologists who have written about the gift relationship in archa-

ic societies have agreed with Hegel and company about the
close reciprocity between private property and personality, but
they have tended to see the connection as one that holds only
within certain cultural boundaries. What is difficult for *us* to
see, they say, are cultures in which, because of the circulation of
the gift, there is neither property nor personality in our sense.
The very cultures that Hegel held to be prehistorical (treating
as he did, Africans and other "native" peoples in the geograph-
ical prelude to his *Philosophy of History*) and that Marx took to
exemplify "primitive communism" (ambiguously designating
either the primary or the undeveloped), the anthropologists
remind us, are much more typical of the human than is the
West, simply because there are so many more of the former.
And as they go on to point out, if the connection between property and personality is a culturally limited fact, then economies
of the gift may carry with them different conceptions of human
beings in the place that *we* allot to subjectivity, individuality,
and personality.

My strategy in *Alcyone* is to suggest that Nietzsche, whose
mind was always on the archaic (most obviously on the Greece
of the *arché*), came to some insights concerning the gift that bear
remarkable parallels to those of the anthropologists. This
should not be a complete surprise because Nietzsche and the
anthropologists, as Jacques Derrida reminds us, launched
almost simultaneous projects aimed at showing that the most
fundamental Western concepts and values were the peculiar
habits of a particular *ethnos*.[2] In *Beyond Good and Evil*, Nietzsche
describes philosophizing as "a kind of atavism of the highest
order" because it consists in tracing out the affiliations of concepts that have grown up in the same cultural milieu. The principles of such affiliation are what Nietzsche calls grammar, and
as an "old philologist" he knows above all that languages are
different and cannot be taken as copies at various removes of
some fundamental *Ursprache* (in the way that, for example, an
earlier philosophical philology had taken Hebrew to be the
source of all languages):

> The strange family resemblance of all Indian, Greek and
> German philosophizing is explained easily enough. Where

there is affinity of languages, it cannot fail, owing to the common philosophy of grammar—I mean, owing to the unconscious domination and guidance by similar grammatical functions—that everything is prepared at the outset for a similar development and sequence of philosophical systems; just as the way seems barred against certain other possibilities of world-interpretation. It is highly probable that philosophers within the domain of the Ural-Altaic languages (where the concept of the subject is least developed) look otherwise "into the world," and will be found on paths of thought different from those of the Indo-Germanic peoples and the Muslims: the spell of certain grammatical functions is ultimately also the spell of *physiological* valuations and racial conditions. (*BGE,* 20; *5,* 34–35)

Yet what is *in* any language, or as some would ask, what is *given* in it? Nietzsche's emphasis on "grammar" in the passage quoted suggests the synchronic approach to language of structural linguistics. Now to be concerned with the archaic is to look not only at the distant other but at possibilities implicit within a certain language or cultural formation that may now be obscured or disguised. This is to indicate the direction of Heidegger's interrogations of the languages of thinking and poetry, and most notably for my purposes, of his attempt to make the simple *"es gibt"* (or in its anglophone philosophical analogue, "the given") resound in a certain way. Heidegger appears to be more interested in archaic origins than in archaic structures. Like Nietzsche, and perhaps more under his spell in this respect than he is able to acknowledge, Heidegger hears these resonances in the archaic Greek of pre-Platonic thought. He hopes that we can rediscover the strange in the familiar and so asks us to hear some of the oldest sayings of the West in ways that they have not been heard by the scholars or by the philosophical tradition from Plato and Aristotle to Hegel and Nietzsche. In listening to the fragment of Anaximander, allegedly the earliest trace of our inheritance from these archaic thinkers, Heidegger takes pains to reread the clause that can be read as speaking not of giving as such but of exchange, as in young Nietzsche's translation: "Whence things have their origin, there they must also pass away according to necessity; for they must pay penalty (*Büsse zahlen*) and be judged for their injustice, according to the ordinance of time."[3] From this saying Heidegger excludes the apparent reference to an economy of exchange and instead substitutes a discourse of usage, jointure, and reck (*Brauch, Fug,* and *Ruch*), that would refer us to a giving beyond all economies. Part of this gesture of translation no doubt consists in turning away from those conventional histories of early Greek philosophy that would remind us of the intimate connection in which the Milesian thinkers Thales, Anaximander, and Anaximenes stood to the active and cosmopolitan commercial life of their time. There perhaps is a desire here to preserve the authenticity and distance of such thinking from a vulgarized culture of the market. But might Heidegger have concluded too hastily that all economies, whether in the common or the metaphysical sense, must be founded on the alienation of goods and the conventions of private property? If that is so, it might help to account for the common feeling that there is something vague and empty in Heidegger's talk of *es gibt.* This giving in which there is no subject, no circulation, and no articulation of a structure in which gifts might be exchanged, comes to appear as a determined flight from the modern market.[4] If Heidegger sometimes opposes to the world of commodified exchange a certain appeal to preindustrial conditions of peasant agriculture and handicraft, we could ask why his range of cultural options is so narrow, and why the peasant life on the land that he evokes is still implicitly committed to an economy of private ownership.

Not only in his early lectures on the Greek thinkers but also in *Thus Spoke Zarathustra,* Nietzsche too alludes to Anaximander's saying, although in the latter case the author's name is not mentioned because the saying is meant to stand for an entire philosophical tradition from the early Greeks down to Schopenhauer. Significantly this reprise of the saying occurs at a point where Zarathustra is discussing the general law of compensation (in a spirit that is not foreign to Emerson's consideration of the same topic); and it is recalled at a time when Zarathustra's hesitations in speaking and articulating his own teaching or gift become obvious. In "Of Redemption" (*Von der*

Erlösung), *redemption* carries with it both its economic and its
religious senses, senses that (as Nietzsche will argue in *Toward
a Genealogy of Morals*) ought to be seen in their complicity.
Should cripples be redeemed? Do their deformities and suffering warrant their receiving compensation and being made right
or whole? To answer such questions in the affirmative is to sub-
scribe to the thirst for revenge against "time and its 'it was'"
that infects many more than just those who happen to be physi-
cally crippled. The principle of such revenge is now attributed
to madness, and to a madness that came into being as part of a
global climatic shift in Western thinking:

> And then cloud upon cloud rolled over the spirit: until at
> last madness preached: "Everything passes away, there-
> fore everything deserves to pass away!
> "And that law of time, that time must devour her chil-
> dren, is justice (*Gerechtigkeit*)": thus madness preached.
> "Things are ordered morally according to justice and
> punishment (*Sittlich sind die Dinge geordnet nach Recht und
> Strafe*). Oh, where is redemption (*Erlösung*) from the
> stream of things and from the punishment 'existence'?
> Thus madness preached. (Z, 162; 4, 180)

Heidegger wanted to preserve a certain insight into pri-
mordial giving by attributing a large part of the traditional
Anaximander saying to later accretions that already derived
from Platonic and Aristotelian thought, providing him with a
radical vantage point from which to assess Western metaphysics. Nietzsche, however, offers an even more sweeping and
radical critique of that tradition to the extent that even Anaximander can be seen as preaching its madness. If there are other
voices, voices that do not preach, but resonate in other keys and
with other words, they too might be found at archaic levels,
such as those that Heidegger explores, but they may be voices
quite distinct from the Anaximander painfully reconstructed
and deconstructed by Heidegger.

In the chapter on gifts I attempt to explore some of the
sounds and voices that resonate through Nietzsche's texts
when we attempt to read them with the metaphysical tradition

in question. All these voices could be said to be archaic inspira-
tions, but to speak of the archaic is simultaneously to suggest
that Nietzsche can be read in the light of rather contemporary
concerns and speculations having to do with economies, the
parasitic relation, and the question of gender. It would be
unfortunate, however, if Nietzsche were construed as on a nostalgic quest for a return to lost origins; rather the archaic
appears in his work as a suggestion of possibilities excluded by
what we have come to call the metaphysics of presence.

If the gift can be said to be the counterconcept that puts
into question not the legitimacy of property but the implicit
universality of the concept of property, similar observations can
be made about noise in relation to language and music and
about women in relation to a putatively universal concept of
man or humanity. Noise is by definition, it seems, arbitrary
sound, especially the sounds made by unwanted intruders or
thoughtless neighbors, animal or human. As such it is opposed
to both discursive language and music, each of which has its
own form of order, syntactic or melodic. The traditional hierarchy clearly is at work in Plato's *Republic* when Socrates pro-
nounces a series of exclusions on various forms of *mimesis.* The
series goes from bad to worse: first one must not imitate those
of high station and repute performing ignoble actions; then
they must not imitate women, especially those wailing in the
grip of misfortune or those who are ill, in labor, or in love; finally Socrates summons up with horror the sounds of the universal pantomime who would imitate "'horses neighing, bulls
lowing, the roaring of rivers,the crashing of the sea, thunder,
and everything of the sort—will they imitate them?' 'But' he
said 'They're forbidden to be mad or to liken themselves to the
mad.'"[5] The canon of performance in poetry and music (the
Greek *mousikē*) excludes not only inferior poetic and musical
modes but the inhuman and the subhuman. In *The Birth of
Tragedy* Nietzsche already questioned the logocentrism that
would always make words prior to melody, and so allied himself with Wagner in an attack on the opera in so far as it
remained discursive. But other sounds are evoked in *The Birth
of Tragedy*, perhaps the echoes of those excluded cries of
women, sounds associated with illness, labor, and love. These

are the sounds that burst into the rigorous world subject to Apollinian canons:

> And now let us imagine how into this world, built on mere appearance and moderation and artificially damned up, there penetrated in tones even more bewitching and alluring, the ecstatic sound of the Dionysian festival; how in these strains all of nature's *excess* in pleasure, grief, and knowledge became audible, even in piercing shrieks; and let us ask ourselves what the psalmodizing artist of Apollo, with his phantom harp-sound, could mean in the face of this demonic folk-song! (*BT*, 4; *1*, 40–41)

These sounds are neither speech nor music, but are, as Nietzsche frequently repeats, *ecstatic* and *excessive*. They are superfluous by any measure, yet here a certain conception of truth is noisily overthrown, for as Nietzsche continues, summarizing what he has just said "*Excess* revealed itself as truth." The excessive, the superfluous and the parasitic are affiliated notions in Nietzsche and as we will see, they are all orchestrated or auditory concepts. Yet these auditory excesses have a difficult and complex relation to economic orders. Such unanticipated disruptions (as in the preceding passage) may be described as a gift or a given in a way that Heidegger might endorse. But they also are interruptions and interjections that summon up apparently pejorative terms such as *parasitic*. It's perhaps a question of who's invited to the feast (here the *Dionysusfeier*); elsewhere in *The Birth of Tragedy* the words of modern (pre-Wagnerian) opera are said to be "parasitic" upon the music (*BT* 19, *1*, 126), but Nietzsche in that context is very far from saying of those words that "excess revealed itself as truth." In the next chapter of this book, I examine the general economy of parasitism that structures the fourth part of *Thus Spoke Zarathustra*. This text, itself often dismissed as merely supplementary or parasitic, brings together the themes of noise, interruption, and the seemingly inevitable degeneration of the gift relationship into that of host and parasite. Reading this part of Nietzsche's gift, I suggest, is rather like performing a score and the performance may affect the way we hear such "doctrines" as the thought of eternal recurrence.

Finally it is necessary to ask how we ought to take Nietzsche's own program notes for *Zarathustra*, and especially his
claim that we fail entirely to hear the work properly if we do
not catch its "halcyon tone." This tone, I suggest, is to be understood in terms of the halcyon theme that runs through Greek
and Latin literature. Whereas Nietzsche's invocations of Dionysus and Ariadne can be regarded as the deliberate use of the
classical mythological repertory, his summoning up of Alcyone's fate and her songs seems to be more of an inspiration
from the classical unconscious. (I say *seems* here because of the
many obvious but difficult questions raised by any discussion
of conscious and unconscious composition in Nietzsche's
work.) Alcyone's voice is gendered, and the reproduction of
her cries would seem to violate Socrates' proscription of the
mimesis of women who are "ill, in labor, or in love." So if her
song does resonate through at least some of Nietzsche's writings, it will be necessary to reconsider the question of the metaphysical affiliations of those texts once they are heard with the
accents of love, sorrow, and childbirth. It now appears that the
universal man or humanity of the metaphysical tradition is in
fact a gendered being. We can read the admission of women
into the guardian class of the *Republic* as well as their exclusions as permissible subjects of *mimesis* as strategies for providing *man* and *humanity* with a gender to which women will be
admitted only by surrendering their own voices. Nietzsche's
objections to this duplicitous universalism are well known, but
we only recently have begun to discover that his writings can
be read or played in such a way as to hear some of those tones
as he transgresses so many mimetic canons.

Notes

1. Hegel, *Encylopedia*, pars. 489 and 490; trans. William Wallace,
in *Hegel's Philosophy of Mind* (New York, 1971), p. 244.

2. Jacques Derrida remarks on this coincidence in his essay
"Structure, Sign and Play in the Discourse of the Human Sciences":
"one can assume that ethnology could have been born as a science
only at the moment when a decentering had come about: at the

moment when European culture—and in consequence, the history of metaphysics and its concepts—had been *dislocated*, driven from its locus, and forced to stop considering itself as the culture of reference...there is nothing fortuitous about the fact that the critique of ethnocentrism—the very condition for ethnology—should be systematically and historically contemporaneous with the destruction of the history of metaphysics" in *Writing and Difference*, trans. Alan Bass (Chicago, 1978), p. 282.

3. On Heidegger's evasion of the question of modern work, production and ownership, see Phillippe Lacoue-Labarthe, *Typography: Mimesis, Philosophy, Politics*, ed. Christopher Fynsk (Cambridge, 1989), especially pp. 75–89.

4. Nietzsche, *Philosophy in the Tragic Age of the Greeks*, as translated by David Farrell Krell and Frank Capuzzi in Martin Heidegger, "The Anaximander Fragment" in *Early Greek Thinking* (New York, 1975), p. 13.

5. Plato, *Republic*, 395e–396b. I present only a brief and conventional .account of Plato's restrictions on *mimesis* here to suggest some of the ways in which Nietzsche's writing deviates from one significant set of philosophical canons; in other words I am, for the moment, more interested in how Plato has been read than in attempting a post-Nietzschean reading. For some suggestions concerning the parameters of such a reading, one might begin with Lacoue-Labarthe's *Typography*. Plato himself was not above engaging in lamentation for a lost love, as his epitaph for Dion shows. The epitaph and Plato's apparent recantation of some of the strictures of the *Republic* are cited and discussed in Martha Nussbaum's *The Fragility of Goodness* (New York, 1986), pp. 200–233.

On Presents and Presence:
The Gift in *Thus Spoke Zarathustra*

One can say with total security that there is nothing
fortuitous about the fact that the critique of ethnocentrism—the very condition for ethnology—should be
systematically and historically contemporaneous with
the destruction of the history of metaphysics.

> —Jacques Derrida "Structure, Sign and Play in
> the Discourse of Human Sciences"

Setting prices, determining values, contriving equivalences, exchanging—these preoccupied the earliest
thinking of man to so great an extent that in a certain
sense they constitute thinking *as such...*

> —*Toward a Genealogy of Morals*, II, 8

Nietzsche warned us that it would be difficult to read *Thus
Spoke Zarathustra*. He told Heinrich von Stein, who had complained that he did not understand a word of the book, that
"having understood six sentences from it—that is, to have really experienced them—would raise one to a higher level of existence than 'modern' men could attain" (*EH*, 259; 6, 299). In the
"Foreword" to *Ecce Homo* he says that with *Zarathustra* he has
"given mankind the greatest present (*Geschenk*) that has been
made to it so far" (*EH*, 219; 6, 259). So Nietzsche claims to have

made us a present, a gift, an offer that we can't understand, and the language of gift-giving suggests that he expects a certain gratitude in return. The gift, giving, exchange, the *es gibt*—all these, we'll soon see, are repeated themes in *Zarathustra*. But I want to begin by considering the way in which Nietzsche articulates these dimensions of *Zarathustra* in *Ecce Homo*. Perhaps, if this may be said without *hubris* (although how avoid *hubris* here?) we may now be in a position to begin to think about a few sentences from this uncanny text for all and none.

In the last section of the Foreword to *Ecce Homo* Nietzsche makes three observations about *Zarathustra* or, what is the same thing, issues three protocols concerned with how the book should be read. The *first*, which I already have quoted, tells us that it is *"das grosste Geschenk"* ever given to mankind, in so far as it is the highest book, a book of the heights. The *second* observation or protocol, which in a way follows from the first, is that everything depends on the ear with which one hears the tone that comes from the mouth that speaks here: *Man muss vor Allem den Ton, der aus diesem Mund kommt, diesen halkyonischen Ton richtig hören, um den Sinn seiner Weisheit nicht erbarmunswürdig Unrecht zu tun* ("Above all one must *hear* aright the tone that comes from his mouth, the halcyon tone, lest one should do wretched injustice to the meaning of its wisdom"). We cannot accept a gift that we cannot hear. One who "hears aright" will not, for example, confuse this voice with that of a prophet. *Third*, Nietzsche anticipates a question, "Is not Zarathustra in view of all this a *seducer*?" That is, if hearing correctly means that one is forced to attune oneself in a certain way, should the process of hearing and reading then be described as the deployment of a strategy, rhetorical and erotic, such that simply listening to the offer or considering the present captivates the reader or listener unawares? To this Nietzsche replies, as he does so frequently in analogous circumstances, by quoting one of Zarathustra's speeches. The speech at the end of "The Gift-Giving Virtue" (*"Die schenkende Tugend"*) concludes the first part of the book, the same speech (I will not repeat here all of Nietzsche's repetition) in which Zarathustra says to his disciples "One repays a teacher badly if one always remains nothing but a pupil. And why do you not want to pluck at my wreath?"

All of these protocols have to do with the thematics and dynamics of giving and receiving. The first tells us what *Thus Spoke Zarathustra* is: it is a gift—the greatest one yet. Do we know how Nietzsche thinks the gift? Or must we read *Zarathustra*, which begins with an invocation of the endlessly giving sun and ends with a party or potlatch that Zarathustra throws or "gives" for the higher men, a party that blows them all away, to see what might be involved in giving and receiving gifts? And what might we make of the statement in the interleaf page of *Ecce Homo* where he names three books as "presents" (*Geschenke*) of the last year or even of its last quarter? Who was the giver if Nietzsche was the receiver? He asks a question whose emphasis suggests that it is more than rhetorical: "How could I fail to be grateful to my own life?" In the case of a great gift from an identifiable other, one certainly could ask "how could I fail to be grateful?" that is, would it not be ignoble not to show the proper thanks? But when the gift's source is not so clear one might ask "*how* can I be grateful—or fail to be grateful?" *How* does one give to oneself, or more precisely, how does one's *life* give something to one and then how does one respond? *Ecce Homo* offers something of an answer to this last question: Nietzsche expresses his gratitude by telling or narrating his life to himself. And is the book that constitutes that telling another gift? Is it to be ascribed to the same "life" that Nietzsche is grateful to, thus increasing his debt, or is it rather his gift in return, perhaps the last gift in a cycle of exchanges? Odd questions that we must begin to attempt to circumscribe and articulate.

The *second* protocol of the Foreword cautions us about the *reception* of what we hear. Something is said but it is unclear whether the sayer is Zarathustra or Nietzsche, however, we will perceive it correctly only if we catch its precise tone. We might note that perceiving, *Wahrnehmen* (as its construction in several languages suggests), always is a kind of *receiving* or taking. Moreover, in these enigmatic protocols, which may share in the ambivalence we so often find characterizing the gift, Nietzsche advises us *how* the book's tone should be characterized; that is, how we ought to hear it. The tone that comes from the mouth, the nonprophetic tone, is "the halcyon tone." I want to defer the discussion of what the *halcyon* means in Nietzsche's texts. But let us note now that it has to do with a story of passion, death, metamorphosis, giving, and receiving that go beyond the episodic or individual level to the cyclical marking or transformation of space and time. Let us recall that Alcyone who gives her name to "the halcyon," was transformed into a sea bird when she desperately willed to follow Ceyx, her drowned husband. And as a result of this transformation the sea observes an annual period of calm each year so that the halcyon (kingfisher) birds can hatch their eggs in those miraculous floating nests described by such ancient authorities as Aristotle, Plutarch, and Ovid. Later we will ask to what extent Nietzsche's naming of the halcyon tone is also a naming of Alcyone and her destiny.

The *third* protocol warns us against a misapprehension. It seems to repeat that contempt for a merely passive, receptive reader expressed in "On Reading and Writing" where Zarathustra says that he "hates the reading idler" (Z 67, 4, 48). It reminds us that Zarathustra rejects any simple discipleship and promises to return to his then-disciples only when they have turned away from him. But we should also attend to the strategy of Nietzsche's citation here. From the book that he has just called the *greatest present* ever given to mankind, he has quoted some of Zarathustra's discourse on *"die schenkende Tugend. "* He chooses to remind the readers of *Ecce Homo* of a text in which Zarathustra: (1) receives a gift from his disciples upon leaving them; (2) offers an interpretation of the gift itself; (3) expounds the supremacy of the gift-giving virtue; and (4) issues the warning quoted, which, in effect, distinguishes the seductive use of gifts from some other social form or practice (let us temporarily call it the practice of a *certain reciprocity*, although it is a reciprocity whose terms are yet to be discovered).

The question of the gift, then, is internal to the text of *Zarathustra*. So we will want to know what it is to be a gift, to be a giver, to be a receiver—and these are questions that arise throughout the book (a gift for all and none).[1] It will be useful to recall some of the ways in which giving and everything associated with it are clearly problematized within the text. For example (but it is more than an example) in the series of economic speeches in which he weighs and measures the "three evils"—sex, the lust to rule, and selfishness—Zarathustra considers each of these both in the "evil" form in which it is conventionally stigmatized and the transvalued form in which it appears to him after his return home, the return in which he now finds his own language. Of the lust to rule (*Herrschsucht*), he says

> The lust to rule—but who would call it *lust* (*Sucht*) when what is high longs downward for power? Verily, there is nothing diseased or lustful in such longing and condescending. That the lonely heights should not remain lonely and self-sufficient eternally; that the mountain should descend to the low plains—oh, who were to find the right name for such longing? "Gift-giving virtue"—thus Zarathustra once named the unnameable. (Z, 208, 4, 238)

Let us think for a moment about the frame within which Zarathustra speaks of naming the unnameable. Like so many of Zarathustra's speeches, it is a report on a dream, "the last dream of the morning" when he "stood in the foothills" and "beyond the world, held scales, and weighed the world." So Zarathustra will be giving us a report on what we will provisionally (and only provisionally) call the *value of the world*. However, from the very beginning this evaluation, this morning stock market report on the value of the world's values, is tinged with a sense of the problematic character of the enterprise of weighing the world. Perhaps this idea of weighing, which involves measure and comparison, was suggested (Zarathustra guesses) by his own day wisdom. For if measuring and weighing have something pinched and prosaic about them, the idea of a total weighing and measuring of the world is dreamlike. (Blake said "Bring out number, weight and measure in a year of dearth.") Weighing the world stands somewhere between dreaming and waking. This project requires that the world be thought of as measurable and in some sense quantifiable. It requires, as Zarathustra says, a mockery of all "infinite worlds." If the world were infinite, or if there were indeed an infinity of worlds, measuring and weighing would be subject to a radical indeterminacy. But here, at least for day wisdom, the principle is: "Wherever there is force, *number* will become mistress: She has more force." What is weighed, then, is "this finite world." *This* world: the actual world of our hopes, regrets, dreams, and experience. This *finite* world: only the finite can be measured.

In this context Zarathustra recalls that he once named the longing of the lonely heights as the *gift-giving virtue (die schenkende Tugend)*. When he did so he was naming the unnamable. But why is it unnameable? Perhaps it is significant that Marcel Mauss says something similar in his *Essay on the Gift*. Mauss argues that gift giving, exchange, and potlatch are totalistic phenomena of archaic cultures that cannot be understood in terms of the individualistic and economistic categories of modern rationality. The practices connected with the gift, its exchange, and circulation are unnameable within a social and economic order assuming the priority of private accumulation and possession; in such a context the gift is an occasional matter, an exception reserved for holidays and special events rather than the very nerve of communal life. The crowd in the marketplace, to whom Zarathustra first attempts to give his gift, can understand neither him nor the practice and discourse within which such giving is possible. The last man is the ultimate creature of the marketplace with his "little pleasure for the day and his little pleasure for the night." When Zarathustra presents what should be a horrifying picture of the last man to the people in the marketplace they ask for *this* gift, not that of the *Übermensch*. In fact they offer a deal, an exchange: "'Give us this last man, Zarathustra,' they cried, 'make us into this last man! You can keep the superman!'" ("*So schenken wir den Übermenschen!*") (Z, 47; 4, 20).

In Nietzsche the failure to understand and the gap between speaker and hearer typically is situated in the marketplace. That is where the madman appears one morning to announce the death of God; while the stock market thinks that it already has discounted its values in anticipation of this information, the madman is telling the traders that they have yet to understand. He ends his day not on the floor of the exchange, but in the churches, singing requiems for the dead God (*GS,*

125; 3, 482). Not only is gift giving (which I will use as a kind of abbreviation for all the associated practices) unnameable from the perspective of the market, but if it should be named, as it is by the Kwakiutl or the Melanesians, for example, then our own moral categories treating of property and individuality would be put in question. Such groups typically have "only a single word to cover buy and sell, borrow and lend.... Concepts which we like to put in opposition—freedom and obligation; generosity, liberality, luxury on the one hand and saving, interest, austerity on the other—are not exact and it would be well to put them to the test."[2] As an example of this confounding of categories Mauss says something that recalls Zarathustra's equation of *Herrschsucht* and *schenkende Tugend*. In what has now become an anthropological commonplace he observes that "Even the destruction of wealth does not correspond to the complete disinterestedness which one might expect." Despite the appearance of mad, frenzied destruction, of "wasteful expenditure" these activities are not disinterested: "Between vassals and chiefs, between vassals and their henchmen, the hierarchy is established by means of these gifts. To give is to show one's superiority.... To accept without returning is to face subordination."[3] As Jacques Derrida observes in *Spurs*, with reference to Mauss and the Maussian tradition, taking this gift giving seriously could lead to alternatives to the Western economico-metaphysical tradition that valorizes individuals and their property and that continues to flourish in an implicit form in Heidegger's thought of the giving in *es gibt* and of the *Eigentum* in *das Ereignis*.[4]

Let us say then that gift giving is unnameable for complex reasons. It is unnameable from within a culture based on private property, the market, and quantifiable exchange. As contemporary anthropologists point out with respect to the work of pioneers such as Mauss, to speak of cultures dominated by ceremonial exchange in terms of the gift runs the risk of superimposing our own social categories on the Melanesians or the Kwakiutl. For we have reserved a certain place for the gift in which it plays the role of that which is *other* than our standard or normal form of dealing with goods, property, and people; gift giving has specific functions within an economy of com-

modities. We run the risk, in transferring this economic anomaly to those who are other than we are (our anthropological others), of seeing them in terms of our own ceremonies. But the
Melanesians (for example) are not celebrating a constant round
of birthday parties. Whatever name we give to gift giving we
ought to be aware that we are risking a deformation of social
categories. And for that matter, what is involved in the anthropologist "giving" a name to the practices of people in another
culture? This giving, especially when done on a global scale, as
we name the life of the other, itself may have some of the
aggressive features of the potlatch or of a Nietzschean "lust to
rule," except that the "beneficiaries," in this case, have no
access to the means of global communication that would allow
them to "return" the gift.

"From Mauss to Lévi-Strauss" (as Merleau-Ponty says),
from Mauss to Bataille to Derrida, the gift, expenditure, or
dépense, the general economy have been proposed as names of
the unnameable and these names sometimes have been used to
read Nietzsche differently, especially by Bataille and those who
have taken him seriously, including Foucault, Derrida, Baudrillard, and Deleuze and Guattari. Of course these thinkers are
hardly in agreement concerning Nietzsche or with regard to the
Maussian themes affiliated with the gift, and if one speaks of a
"Maussian tradition" (as I did just now) it must be recognized
that the bonds and affiliations are genealogical rather than
axiomatic.[5] There would be evident here, if one wished to ana-
lyze it, a complex network of gifts and exchanges, of antioedipal
potlatches in which Nietzsche circulates as a gift only to be disseminated or deconstructed. And because in the circular ontolo-
gy of the world of the gift, what goes around comes around,
Nietzsche receives and suffers as much as he gives and inspires.

The complexity of gift giving already is announced and
enacted at the beginning of *Thus Spoke Zarathustra.* In the generalized economy of gift giving the gift is "for all and none," so it
is put into circulation, and eventually it passes through the
entire social world; but it is destined to be a permanent possession for none (in gift giving societies the corresponding status
may be marked by the complete wasting, destruction, or expenditure of the object in question). In the *Vorrede,* Zarathustra's

first speech is to the sun, whom he personifies and praises for his *schenkende Tugend:* "You great star, what would your happiness be had you not those for whom you shine?" And Zarathustra too is overfull: "Behold, I am weary of my wisdom, like a bee that has gathered too much honey; I need hands outstretched to receive it. "

"I would give away and distribute (*verschenken und austeilen*), until the wise among men find joy once again in their folly, and the poor in their riches" (Z, 39; 4, 11). *Verschenken und austeilen:* these name the processes of expenditure that constitute Zarathustra's *Untergehen* among men. To live in solitude, as Zarathustra has done for ten long years, is *not* to give, but his entrance into society must be marked by gift giving. And at the same time that he praises the sun, who always gives and never receives, he names the deficiency, the vice that corresponds to the gift-giving virtue: "So bless me then, you quiet eye that can look upon an all-too-great-happiness without envy (*Neid*)!" Envy, we learn later (for example, in "On the Tree on the Mountainside"), is a disease of the eye, the evil eye that characterizes the economic stance of the resentful who practice a morality of good and evil. When Zarathustra confesses to envy in "The Night Song," it is a complex, paradoxical envy of the receiver by the giver; he longs to surrender his blazing light to accept another's gifts.

Those who live alone exist in a precarious and sensitive relation to the modalities of giving and receiving exemplified by the extremes of the quiet or the evil eye. The evil eye, we could say, would destroy a good thing or another's happiness not in a spirit of festive expenditure and not to take possession of it for itself but simply to free itself from the pain caused by that good or by the happiness of another.[6] It is worth noting, then, that Zarathustra's first contact, after his solitary silence, is with a hermit who recognizes him by the purity of his eyes: "*Ja, ich erkenne Zarathustra. Rein ist sein Auge und an seinen Munde birgt sich keine Ekel.*" "Yes, I recognize Zarathustra. His eye is pure and no disgust lurks about his mouth." That Zarathustra will later express envy of a sort and plumb the depths of nausea and disgust ought not to obscure the importance of the hermit's identifying Zarathustra as one who is fit to give and

receive. This is Zarathustra's first conversational exchange and
the subject is the varieties of exchange itself. *Why* does
Zarathustra go down to men, to "sleepers," demands the hermit. Zarathustra's first answer is "I love man," but the hermit
easily replies that love of man is precisely *his* reason for having
retreated into his solitude: man is unworthy of love, love of
man would be fatal for him. Zarathustra's self-correction is
speedy: "Did I speak of love? I bring men a gift (*ein Geschenk*)"
(Z, 40; 4, 13).

There is much to think about in this contrast between love
and gift giving. Perhaps the most obvious implication is that
the gift always may be ambiguous; it may not be, and perhaps
never is, the correlate of a purely disinterested act of bestowing.
The gift places the recipient under an obligation, an obligation
burdensome in proportion to its value. This is one of those
valuable principles of worldly wisdom that can be derived
from the aphorisms of books such as *Human, All Too Human*
and *Daybreak*. And we might wonder, if *Thus Spoke Zarathustra*
itself is to be regarded as the greatest gift ever given to humanity, under what obligations of reciprocity does it place humanity,
and how ought we to respond to the gift? Clearly the gift that
Zarathustra has in mind is not one that will be received with
ease. In fact it is hardly clear at this early point in the story
what that gift is and whether Zarathustra himself has a clear
and constant conception of what he will be giving. If the gift is
the thought of the *Übermensch* or that of eternal recurrence then
we may wonder if Zarathustra knows yet just what those gifts
are. To accept such gifts requires some understanding of them,
an understanding clearly lacking in the people Zarathustra
addresses in the marketplace. But if they were to accept such
gifts, gifts that carry with them abysmal thoughts, they would
have to go under, as Zarathustra tells them. The gift-giving
virtue *is* the lust to rule.

Zarathustra's entire exchange with the hermit articulates
these ambiguities of the gift relationship. And of course as an
exchange it also exemplifies these very same ambiguities, for
Zarathustra is a speaker and what he has to give are his words.
That we call conversation *exchange* suggests that there is an *economics* of speech as well as a grammar and a rhetoric.

"Give them nothing!" said the saint. Rather take something off them and bear it with them—that will please them best; if only it be pleasing to you! And if you want to give to them, give no more than alms, and let them beg for that!" "No," answered Zarathustra. "I give no alms. I am not poor enough for that."

It is worth noticing that Zarathustra simply ignores the suggestion that he ought to take part of men's load from them. Later, however, in the chapter "Of Redemption" he replies to a hunchback who has asked why Zarathustra will not perform miraculous cures. There he explains that to take the hump away from the hunchback, to lighten his load, would be to take his spirit from him. But Zarathustra does reply to the hermit's suggestion that he make men beg for alms. That would be a kind of poverty, for it would presuppose that one did not have the strength and riches for a fuller exchange. The hermit knows that Zarathustra's entrance into society will be difficult. If he has treasures (*Schätze*) to give he must beware of men's wariness in accepting them, for they are "mistrustful of hermits" and will more readily see them as thieves than as benefactors. That is, gifts and exchange are expected; they form the very principle of sociality when there is some tie or ongoing communication among people. The outsider will be feared as a thief. How should we understand the encounter of the two hermits, Zarathustra on his way down to man and the saint who, as he explains himself, praises god by "singing, crying, laughing, and humming" in the forest? And despite the hermit's apparent self-sufficiency he expects something from Zarathustra for he asks "what do you bring us as a gift?" However, Zarathustra is all discretion and leaves quickly so as not to take anything from this hermit who has yet to hear that God is dead. By echoing the simplest question of the child to a parent returning from a trip—"what did you bring me?"—the hermit shows how difficult it is to be truly isolated. The gift economy is ready to be activated at any time. And Zarathustra observes at least one principle of hospitality by discreetly refusing to disillusion his host. This first conversational exchange is an artful exercise in diplomacy; words are skillfully deployed to ensure that the balance remains what it was before the encounter.

Questions have been raised, however, by Zarathustra's meeting with the hermit. The encounter could be taken as Nietzsche's transformation of the fable of the state of nature. Two isolated figures meet, figures who as hermits are represented as self-sufficient. But they enact neither the Hobbesian war of all against all nor the Hegelian battle to the death that is resolved only through the elementary social form of lord and bondsman. Instead they engage in a highly ceremonial and subtly orchestrated discussion of gifts, in which each verbal gesture is a giving or a receiving. Of course that analogy with the state of nature is deceiving, for both Zarathustra and the old hermit are themselves voluntary exiles from the world of men. Yet standing at the verge of Zarathustra's story, this meeting can be taken as emblematic. It provides a view of the social relation that implicitly rejects a political economy or anthropology that assumes the priority of rational, self-interested individuals.

Giving and receiving are both fraught with danger. *Die schenkende Tugend,* like other virtues, requires courage. Nietzsche read this in Emerson (whose essay "Gifts" is cited by Mauss as an anticipation of his own anthropological insights). Certainly a careful reading of "Gifts" would both help to alter the still popular picture of Emerson as a cheery and superficial sage (humming to God in the forest) and would demonstrate the ground of the elective affinity Nietzsche discovered with the American philosopher. Emerson writes that

> The law of benefits is a difficult channel, which requires careful sailing, or rude boats. It is not the office of a man to receive gifts. How dare you give them? We wish to be self-sustained. We do not quite forgive a giver. The hand that feeds us is in some danger of being bitten. We can receive anything from love, for that is a way of receiving it from ourselves; but not from any one who assumes to bestow.[7]

For Emerson both giving and receiving entail risks and are capable of multiple forms of perversion and degradation. Giving itself is degraded when one substitutes a commodity expressly designed to be given for the true gift. Emerson admonishes us that "Rings and other jewels are not gifts, but apologies for gifts. The only gift is a portion of thyself. Thou must bleed for me." He seems to recognize that gift giving is seen by both giver and recipient as a sign of power, or of the *Herrschsucht* that for Nietzsche is its other name. So, for example, "[y]ou cannot give anything to a magnanimous person. After you have served him he at once puts you in debt by his magnanimity."[8] Gift giving risks undermining the masks, as Nietzsche calls them, that are necessary for our protection. In giving a gift one undertakes the hermeneutical project of discovering what is appropriate to the true character of the recipient. If I fail to interpret him properly, he will feel that some violence or degradation has been done; but if the donor succeeds in reading the heart of the donee the latter may feel that his private space has been invaded and his very joy at the gift will confirm the donor in his interpretation of the man behind the mask. Some of the bi- or multivalence of giving is apparent in Nietzsche's notes from the time of the composition of Zarathustra:

> It's more than a matter of giving: it's also a matter of creating and violence (*Vergewaltigen*)! The essential thought of the second solitude (beginning of III)
> Our "gifts" (*Geschenke*) are dangerous. (*10, 512*)[9]

And in a note entitled "Plan for *Zarathustra* III" he writes "giving (*das Schenken*) transforms itself—from giving (*Geben*) arose the practice of forcing someone to receive (*Zwang-zum-Nehmen*)" (*10, 516*). In the next sentence Nietzsche writes of "the tyranny of the artist," suggesting that we ought not to suppose that the artist is simply a spontaneous giver; in his giving there is also a withholding and a violent imposition.

Nietzsche often expresses his sense of indebtedness and gratitude to Emerson. Perhaps a large part of the substance of that debt is a complex of themes drawn from economic thought, taken in the most comprehensive sense: debt, gifts, compensation, squandering, and the like. The external signs of indebtedness have been noted several times, and the spirit of the relation is captured in two jottings from the time of *The Gay Science:*

1. *Emerson.*—Never have I felt so much at home in a book,
   and in *my* home, as—I may not praise it, it is too close
   to me. (*9, 588*)

2. The author who has been richest in ideas in this century has so far been an American (unfortunately made
   obscure by German philosophy—frosted glass).[10]

The first statement locates the relationship within an order of
respect, nobility, honor, and exchange. To praise Emerson would
be to praise himself; here in the privacy of his notes Nietzsche
forbears to do what he does as public thinking in works such as
Ecce Homo. The second note tells us that Nietzsche does not find
Emerson's riches in a recycling of German philosophy, as some
commentators have suggested. According to those accounts,
Emerson would simply have been the medium by which Nietzsche could draw on his own national heritage, a heritage that
he could not explicitly accept because of his polemics against
the theological prejudices of Kant, Hegel, and their philosophical kin. Nietzsche's notes for *The Gay Science* and *Thus Spoke
Zarathustra* are full of references to Emerson and citations from
his *Essays.* Very often the same notebook entry will contain such
references along with specific plans for one of these books. Let
us explore one of these sketches for it suggests something of the
economies of friendship, the gift, and the state.

> Zarathustra recognizes that he is also not there for his
> friends "Who are my friends?" Neither for the people, nor
> for individuals. *Neither for the many nor for the few! Friend-
> ship is to be overcome! Signs* of self-overcoming at the begin-
> ning of III.
> Emerson p. 426 description of the wise man. (*10, 512*)

The passage from Emerson's essay "Politics" is a long one
but it displays both the non-Germanic character of the riches
Nietzsche finds in Emerson and themes that are recognizable in
the published text of *Zarathustra* III.

> Hence the less government we have the better—the fewer
> laws, and the less confided power. The antidote to this

abuse of formal Government is the influence of private character, the growth of the Individual; the appearance of the principal to supersede the proxy; the appearance of the wise man; of whom the existing government is, it must be owned, but a shabby imitation. That which all things tend to educe; which freedom, cultivation, intercourse, revolutions, go to form and deliver, is character; that is the end of nature, to reach unto this coronation of her king. To educate the wise man the State exists, and with the appearance of the wise man the State expires. The appearance of character makes the State unnecessary. The wise man is the State. He needs no army, fort, or navy—he loves men too well; no bride, or feast, or palace, to draw friends to him; no vantage ground, no favorable circumstance. He needs no library, for he has not done thinking; no church, for he is a prophet; no statute-book, for he has the lawgiver; no money, for he is value; no road, for he is at home where he is; no experience, for the life of the creator shoots through him, and looks from his eyes. He has no personal friends, for he who has the spell to draw the prayer and piety of all men unto him need not husband and educate a few to share with him a select and poetic life. His relation to men is angelic; his memory is myrrh to them; his presence, frankincense and flowers.[11]

Recall that *Zarathustra* III, whose sketch cites this Emersonian passage, portrays a long journey of homecoming in which Zarathustra progressively takes his leave of various forms of social and political life with which he first became engaged in going down to men after a ten years' solitude and then in a second sojourn after a dream came to warn him that his teaching was in danger. When Zarathustra the wise finally comes home to himself he rejoices that he no longer needs to speak the distorting language of the crowd (in "The Homecoming") and he struggles silently with his most abysmal thought, after which he breaks out into a series of songs for which there is no audience of friends or spectators. Of the wise man Emerson says that "he has no personal friends" because he has "the spell to draw the prayer and piety of all men unto him," a formula that could describe the way in which the higher men seek out Zarathustra in the last part of Nietzsche's book. The wise man is portrayed as beyond the contractual requirements of the state and the money economy. His "presence" to men takes the form of presents: "His relation to men is angelic; his memory is myrrh to them; his presence, frankincense and flowers." In the next few sentences Emerson adds that Malthus and Ricardo, that is the theorists of political economy, have no way of recording or even suspecting the existence of the "presence" of character. As angelic the wise man is a gift, a luminous visitation. Emerson discusses the nature of this gift in his essay on that subject. Although his advice there that "Flowers and Fruits are always fit presents" may sound like a simpering cliche, the reason adduced is one that shows a rigorous economic logic:

> flowers, because they are a proud assertion that a ray of beauty outvalues all the utilities of the world.... Fruits are acceptable gifts, because they are the flower of commodities, and admit of fantastic values being attached to them.[12]

In the same essay, however, Emerson notes that once we give gifts of a more specific nature by which we aim at discerning or matching the particular character of our friends, we enter into a risky business in which the receiver may feel offended either by our failure to understand him or by our having understood him all too well.

Consider the economic thought of Emerson's essay "Compensation," which develops what could be thought of as a general economy of life. The essay begins by arguing against the conventional religious view that there is no justice in this life but that there is an appropriate compensation in the next one. Such a view amounts to a needless doubling of the world, generated by the resentment of those who think that they see the wicked prosper while their own virtue goes unrewarded. It also seems to suggest that the rewards of the virtuous life simply are those things like stocks and champagne denied to the poor in this world. Here Emerson comes close to providing an account of the creation of a fictitious secondary world resembling the one that Nietzsche gives in the first essay of *Toward a*

Genealogy of Morals. It also is suggested that it is possible to affirm this world in all of its variety, with its circulation of credits and debits, without reference to anything beyond or outside it: "Being is the vast affirmative, excluding negation, self-balanced and swallowing up all relations, parts and times within itself." What's most remarkable however in the economic doctrine of "Compensation" is Emerson's prescription of what appears to be an inversion of the debtor-creditor analogy as it applies to man and God: "Put God in your debt. Every stroke shall be repaid. The longer payment is withholden, the better for you; for compound interest on compound interest is the rate and usage of this exchequer."[13] The Christian view, as Nietzsche develops it in the second essay of *Toward a Genealogy of Morals* is that we owe an immeasurable debt to God, one that could not possibly be repaid. God's grace through Christ is equivalent to writing off a bad debt, but it is a forgiveness that leaves the debtors with the feeling that the debt could not possibly have been repaid through their own efforts. In *The Gay Science* Nietzsche is quoting from Emerson's "Gifts" when he says: "*Frankincense.*—Buddha says: 'Do not flatter your benefactors.' Repeat this saying in a Christian church: right away it clears the air of everything Christian" (*GS*, 142; 3, 489).[14] When Zarathustra replies to the hermit, "I give no alms. For that I am not poor enough," we can take him to be commenting on such a completely asymmetric relationship of giver and receiver. When one gives alms, for which one expects no return whatsoever, one humiliates the objects of one's charity by placing them in a situation that emphasizes their impotence and incapacity. Zarathustra's remark says, in effect, that the need to establish such an asymmetry is itself a form of poverty, for one who was rich, strong, and overflowing would take delight in the contest and circulation of gift exchange. The call to "Put God in your debt" is the principle of an economy of excess in which one is willing to compete with the wealthiest. Zarathustra's first speech begins by taking the constantly giving sun as his model; the sun gives to excess, but it also provokes responses in the form of growth, flowering, and energy.

A reading of *Toward a Genealogy of Morals*, a book that also deals with the earliest economic relationships, could lead to the conclusion that Nietzsche explicitly rejects the possibility of an economy of the gift. For there he seems to suggest that the oldest social structures are based on debt and credit, understood not as obligations to exchange gifts, but as relations in which the terms are all capable of being determined as monetary or quasi-monetary equivalents. Proceeding from that principle Nietzsche generates an account of morality, religion, and the state; and he also suggests that philosophy itself is to be understood in this perspective: "Setting prices, determining values, contriving equivalences, exchanging—these preoccupied the earliest thinking of man to so great an extent that in a certain sense they constitute thinking *as such*" (*GM* II, 8; 5, 306). Yet in the same text Nietzsche says in a number of ways that the creditor-debtor relation is equiprimordial with other social forms and institutions, claiming that it is "as old as the idea of 'legal subjects' ['*Rechtssubjekte*']" (*GM* II, 4; 5, 298). Here Nietzsche could be construed as making a point similar to Mauss's claim that the very conception of personal and legal subjects is intimately tied to a quantifiable economy of equivalences; as Nietzsche argued in an earlier passage the subject is itself a fiction produced by *ressentiment* (*GM* I, 13; 5, 279). And in the text where Nietzsche speaks of "the earliest thinking of man" he quickly goes on to sketch a view according to which man *came to* call himself *man* (*manas*) or the evaluating one. All of these statements about the emergence of the creditor-debtor relationship, then, seem to allow for at least the possibility of another economy that precedes "legal subjects," "personal legal rights," and even man.

Remembering that *Thus Spoke Zarathustra* itself is said to be the greatest gift ever given to mankind, and keeping in mind the ambivalence of the gift relation, we should be aware that the episodes of the book tend to be framed in a highly charged fashion that may volatilize what circulates through them. Consider the notorious chapter "On Little Women Young and Old." Readers who have taken seriously Nietzsche's curses upon the "idling reader" tend to note that the infamous imperative, "Are you going to women? Don't forget the whip!" is not exactly Zarathustra's own utterance and is even less directly attributable to Nietzsche. It is his citation of what the old woman said to him, and it is delivered in the course of an exchange with a disciple. The framing shows that the stereotypical readings of the episode as crude misogyny may themselves be crude. But it ought to be recognized that both the entire scene and its framing conversation are forms of exchange.

One exchange, between Zarathustra and his disciple, reports another exchange with the little old woman. This is a somewhat ritualistic encounter reminiscent of the meeting with the hermit, except that there is an explicit frame story here that doubles and qualifies the story framed. Zarathustra steals through the twilight, with something concealed under his cloak. The disciple asks whether it is a treasure (*Schatz*) that has been given him, a child born to him, or a stolen object; the question is, To which of these three economic categories does it belong? (Let us not forget that a fine newborn child is a paradigmatic target of the evil eye; it is a natural economic good that must be concealed from the envious.) Zarathustra reveals that it is *both* a treasure and a child. (It's a little bundle, like a book perhaps. And a book, *this one,* is said to be the greatest gift.) How did he acquire it? He had a chance encounter with a little old woman who complains that Zarathustra speaks of everything under the sun except women. Like the hermit, she wants a gift and she recognizes, as perhaps the hermit does not, that Zarathustra's gifts are speeches. In this case Zarathustra does have something to give, although his alacrity in speaking is apparently prompted by the old woman's promise to forget quickly whatever she's told. And she recognizes the obligation to reciprocate, for she asks deliberately whether Zarathustra will accept in return (*nimm zum Dank*) "a little truth." This is considerate because, as we've seen, accepting a gift may be dangerous. But Zarathustra consents to receive it (one of only a very small number of gifts that he does receive) and so he becomes the possessor, for the time being, of the little truth/child/gift: "*Du gehst zu Frauen? Vergiss die Peitsche nicht!*" (Z 83; 4, 86). The saying or the whip itself might be considered an ambivalent gift, with both the bite of poison (like the German *Gift* or *Gabe*) and the capacity for giving pleasure. The personal address—"*Du*"—suggests that this is a gift for Zarathustra in particular, as does the isolated scene of the exchange. Yet just as even the hermit cannot remain aloof from the circle of gifts and exchanges, so such secret gifts tend to become public currency, as Zarathustra passes the treasure on to his disciple and Nietzsche includes it as part of his own double-edged gift to humanity. What is described in Zarathustra's story to his disciple is not an episode of domination, but one of symbolic exchange. The exchange of gifts is of those preeminently symbolic things, words or discourses. Moreover, it is an exchange between genders, a matter that Nietzsche often suggests is both difficult and of the greatest importance. At the beginning of *The Birth of Tragedy*, Nietzsche compares the hostility and infrequent reconciliations of the Apollinian and Dionysian to the war of the sexes. In this context there is also something of a sexual difference between the two gods who give their names to these tendencies, because of Apollo's clearly masculine identity and Dionysus' more androgynous manifestations. Later on in the same text an uneasy truce between the two is described as marked by "a periodical exchange of gifts of esteem" (*periodischer Übersendung von Ehrengeschenken*) (BT 2; 1, 32).

We might compare this exchange of and about the gift with the one in the very next chapter, "On the Adder's Bite," in which Zarathustra first reverses the apparent value of snakebite by claiming that he's been given a gift and then humbles the adder by telling him "take back your poison (*Gift*). You are not rich enough to give it to me" (Z, 93; 4, 87). (Let us remember that the German *Gift* once had the sense of present as well as poison. Nietzsche may very well have been aware of the English homonym of *Gift*. The German translation of Emerson's essay "Gifts," from which Nietzsche quotes in *The Gay Science* is entitled "*Gaben*"; a *Gabe* is either a present or a dose, that is something possibly unpleasant and possibly administered against one's will.) The moral Zarathustra draws from this incident is this: "If you have an enemy, do not requite (*vergeltet*) him evil with good, for that would put him to shame. Rather prove that he did you some good." This teaching of new virtue and its many analogues should be contrasted with the utilitarian economies of the last man, who is a fantasy of and for those who think in the marketplace. They suggest that the dictum *Schätzen ist Schaffen* and Zarathustra's talk of the need to revalue are not simply calls for a shift in what we might designate as the rate of exchange; they are also incitements to *Umwertung*, to transvalue values in a way that defetishizes what has been mystified while opening it up to exchange in a generalized economy.

Consider now Zarathustra's discourse on *"Die schenkende Tugend"* itself, his attempt to name the unnameable.[15] And consider that speech in its narrative context, at the end of the series of speeches that Zarathustra gives in the town called The Motley Cow, which constitute Part I. As the last of these speeches it is a summing up, and a ceremonial speech of departure; one in which the master both takes leave of his disciples and asks them to take leave of him. But not before accepting a farewell gift, for this is an occasion for symbolic exchange. What is that gift? "A staff on whose golden handle a serpent coiled around the sun." Yet this golden globe has not come from nowhere. Zarathustra already has thrown out this ball to open up a game with his disciples. In the speech just before the ritualistic leave-taking, he anticipates a more profound departure by lecturing "On Free Death." Death should be a fulfillment, a consummation, a festival, a gift for the living. It would be the ultimate expenditure, the confirmation of Zarathustra's blessing on those who squander themselves. Earlier he had said to the crowd in the marketplace "I love him whose soul *squanders* (*verschwendet*) itself, who wants no thanks and gives none in return: for he gives continuously and does not want to preserve himself" (Z, 44; 4, 17). And Zarathustra speaks of his own death, a death that he wills so that his friends "may love the earth more," as he says, "for my sake" (Z, 99, 4, 95). A summing up is called for: "Verily, Zarathustra had a goal; he threw his ball: now you my friends are the heirs of my goal; to you I throw my golden ball. More than anything, I like to see you, my friends, throwing the golden ball. And so I will linger a little on the earth: forgive me that." Parenthetically we may note Zarathustra's postponement of his death, a theme carefully explored in David Krell's *Postponements.*[16] Now this postponement is associated with gift giving and exchange. Do the disciples hope to defer Zarathustra's death by engaging him in a cycle of exchanges? Before he can die, leaving them in his debt, they return the golden ball, luring their teacher into a game of catch. He, of course, already had confessed his weakness for watching them at play, but now he will be drawn into the game itself.

In the very next chapter, the disciples throw the ball back into Zarathustra's court with their gift of the staff; it is the golden sun encircled by the serpent. A staff is an appropriate gift for a wandering teacher and mountain climber, and its design exhibits careful thought on the part of the donors. Zarathustra is delighted with this gift, putting it to immediate use by leaning on it. His way of receiving the golden ball, of keeping it in play and circulation, is to interpret it to explain the gift-giving virtue. Here we might stop to ask an apparently very simpleminded question: what is a ball? For it is a ball that Zarathustra and his disciples are tossing back and forth. According to Michel Serres, in *The Parasite:*

> A ball is not an ordinary object, for it is what it is only if a subject holds it. Over there, on the ground, it is nothing; it is stupid; it has no meaning, no function and no value. Ball isn't played alone.... The ball is the quasi-object and quasi-subject by which I am a subject, that is to say, sub-mitted.[17]

This back and forth play of the ball, a play that allows us to become subjects, was also the theme of some of Freud's meditations on play and the compulsion to repeat. These ball games can be attempts to master the threat of absence and death by producing a play of presence and absence, a *fort/da* pattern, that is not simply imposed on the subject but which the subject initiate and sustains.

In the interpretation that Zarathustra tosses back to his disciples he explains that gold has the highest value because it is "uncommon and useless and shining and mellow in lustre" (Z, 100; *4*, 97). It is an image of the highest virtue, a parable or metaphor (*Gleichniss*) of the elevation of body and spirit. And just as the disciples had interpreted Zarathustra through their gift, so he interprets them in commenting on it. "You thirst," he says,

> "to become sacrifices and gifts (*Opfern und Geschenken*) yourselves; and that is why you thirst to heap up all riches in your soul...your virtue is insatiable in wanting to give.

You compel all things to come to you and into you, that
they may flow back from your fountain as gifts of your
love. Truly, such a gift-giving love must approach all values as a robber" (Z, 100; 4, 98).

Notice that Zarathustra tells the disciples that they not only
want to give, in the conventional sense, as in giving him the gift
of the staff, but that they thirst to become "sacrifices and gifts"
themselves.

Here it is important to distinguish two moments or dimensions of gift economy that are only implicitly distinct in the
thought of an anthropologist like Mauss. There is what might be
called the *stabilizing* aspect of gift giving, according to which it
produces and legitimates a regular series of exchanges and
expectations within a community or among communities. Par-
ticipating in regular gift exchanges is a way of knowing who one
is and how one is seen by others. But there also is the dangerous
and transgressive aspect of giving, as in the violence of the potlatch, with its valorization of destruction, waste, and expenditure. The first aspect is surreptitiously identified as the whole of
the practice in Mauss's nostalgic program for a rebirth of a communal spirit in modern society out of the spirit of the gift. In
contrast to such hopes for a humane socialism stands Georges
Bataille's notion of expenditure that focuses on the radicalism of
the potlatch.[18] We might think of the second form, which
Zarathustra seems to attribute to the disciples, as the *Umwertung* of the first. Gold, the sun, Zarathustra, the disciples
(whether they know it or not) are all constituted by a principle
of expenditure that necessarily risks self-destruction. In his
hermeneutic speech on the meaning of the staff, Zarathustra
constructs a proportional metaphor: gold is to the gift-giving
virtue as mind and virtue are to the body. This is both rhetorical-
ly and philosophically familiar. Aristotle praises the cognitive
value of the proportional metaphor; Plato already had deployed
a proportional metaphor in his story about the sun and the
good, initiating a long tradition of philosophical metaphorics.
Yet Zarathustra's use of the form, again employing the figure of
the radiant golden globe, rejects the Platonic notion of the sun as
completely self-sufficient. While the traditional proportional

metaphor of philosophy and theology has as a final term, the Good or God, understood as sheer presence, the final term of Zarathustra's metaphor is the radiant body. But this is not to fantasize the body as a perfect indestructible source of energy. The body of which Zarathustra speaks, the one that gives meaning and direction to those metaphorical chains is one whose elevations are such that it "poetizes and raves and flutters with broken wings" (Z, 60; 4, 36). The body that "flutters with broken wings" can be read as a striking image of sexuality. Raving, poetizing, fluttering with broken wings—these are forms of expenditure, of giving as squandering or *Verschwenden*. Zarathustra has transformed the ritualistic scene of giving a gift to an esteemed teacher into an occasion for praise of an unrestricted giving, what Bataille would call *dépense*.

It is in that light that we can hear the second and third parts of the discourse on *die schenkende Tugend*. In the second, Zarathustra tells his disciples "let the value of all things be posited newly by you!" (*"aller Dinge Werth neu von euch gesetzt!"*) (Z, 102; 4, 100). The language of value and valuation that Nietzsche so often invokes, in contexts ranging from this one to the project of *Umwertung* itself, can be seen as more than the mere residue of the Platonic and metaphysical tradition; that, however, is the way Heidegger pictures such discourse in his polemic against Nietzsche's talk of values. Here Zarathustra sets values and valuation within the context of expenditure and passionate squandering. In the third section of Zarathustra's discourse, we are told that there is yet another change of tone when he admonishes the young men to "lose me and find yourselves." Is this not also a squandering of his disciples, a willingness to let them be dispersed and disseminated rather than identified as his intellectual property? Later Zarathustra will squander or "waste" the higher men whom he assembles at his cave by simply blowing them away.

In addition to "The Gift-Giving Virtue," the other chapter of *Zarathustra* that Nietzsche later cites most extensively is "The Night Song," an episode constituting the solitary inversion of his radiant identification with the sun. "Even the deepest melancholy of such a Dionysus still turns into a dithyramb," he says in *Ecce Homo*. Giving and squandering must have as their constant accompaniment the threat of exhaustion and emptiness and may be the occasion of a corresponding transvaluation of values. "But I live in my own light," Zarathustra laments:

> "But I live in my own light, I drink back into myself the flames that break from me.
>
> I do not know the joy of the receiver; and I have often dreamed that stealing must be more blessed than receiving.
>
> It is my poverty that my hand never rests from giving; it is my envy, that I see expectant eyes and illuminated nights of longing.
>
> Oh wretchedness of all givers! Oh, darkening of my sun! Oh, craving to crave! Oh, ravenous hunger in satiation!" (Z, 129; 4, 136–137)

In *Ecce Homo* Nietzsche tantalizes the reader, after re-citing this, by suggesting that only Ariadne could answer "such a dithyramb of solar solitude" and that only he knows who Ariadne is. Poverty and envy previously had been ascribed to those who had nothing to give; but now we are made aware of the perfectly general aspect of these economic positions by seeing how they can infect the giver, whose "happiness in giving died in giving. "

Zarathustra's struggle with eternal recurrence in "The Convalescent" is preceded by memories of this low point in his career as a giver and followed by a lyrical section where he speaks of a kind of giving that is internal to the soul. Rejoicing in his solitude (*Einsamkeit*), he looks back on the time of "The Night Song" as a period of being forsaken (*Verlassensein*):

> "you sat on your island, a well of wine among empty pails, spending and expending (*schenken und ausschenken*), bestowing and flowing (*gebend und ausgebend*) among the thirsty, until finally you sat thirsty among drunks and complained by night 'Is it not more blessed to receive than to give? And to steal more blessed than to receive?'" (Z, 203; 4, 232)

Wine, we are reminded, is one of the primary things that can be expended and flowing; it is what Dionysus gives and what exhausts Zarathustra in his giving. It is after attaining his own

language in "The Homecoming" that Zarathustra weighs the
world and recounts, in the passage cited earlier, how we had
named the unnameable as the gift-giving virtue.

One way in which one could be both giver and receiver,
sun and darkest night, would be to give to oneself. After the
seizure, the trance, and the rapture recounted in "The Convalescent," Zarathustra chides his animals for misunderstanding
the depth of his thought and experience. But when he finally is
alone, he converses with his own soul "On the Great Longing."
In this extraordinary song, which might bear some comparison
with an Emersonian "Song of Myself," a constantly repeated
refrain is "O my soul, I gave you." These are hard sayings and
difficult songs, for they suppose that the self is not a single
thing, a unit, but a plurality that allows for conversation and
exchange. And Zarathustra sums up the exchange in this way:

> O my soul, I have given you everything, and my hands
> have become empty through you:—and now! now you ask
> me, smiling and full of melancholy, "Which of us owe
> thanks?
>
> Does the giver not owe thanks to the receiver for receiv-
> ing? Is giving not a necessity? Is taking not—compas-
> sion?" (Z, 239; 4, 279)

The exorbitant and excessive nature of this exchange, whose
product is said to be an overfull and overrich soul, is marked by
Zarathustra's invocation of the angels—surely a Nietzschean
anomaly. "The angels," we hear "are themselves melted by tears
because of the overgraciousness of your smile." The soul is so full,
having been given so much, that it begins to think of "the vintager
who is waiting with his diamond knife." Once harvested we can
imagine these grapes fermenting into Dionysian wine that will be
distributed, as we have already heard, and given out in an act of
spending and expending. This entire discourse is to be contrasted
with that of Zarathustra's animals, who would like to put certain
words in his mouth. They would like him to say "*I* come again,"
"*I* spoke my teaching," "*I* break of my teaching," and so on. For
the animals the gift *is* Zarathustra's, for in their understanding, he
is the teacher of eternal recurrence. But in the song "On the Great

Longing" the only teaching and giving that the convalescent acknowledges is one that expansively bursts open the bounds of the soul, one that has made it more "comprehending and comprehensive (*umfangender und umfänglicher*)" than any other soul—its *Umfang* is so great that gifts and thanks can circulate within it. We might read "The Seven Seals" with the same ear, for here Zarathustra speaks of love and the gift of a wedding ring, "the ring of rings, the ring of recurrence" that he is ready to give to eternity. The wedding ring ordinarily is supposed to be a noncirculating gift, and so has a connection with eternity; but here it is noncirculating, we might say, only to the extent that it comprehends recurrence, the circulation of all circulations.

This perhaps is the time to reflect a bit more closely on Heidegger's critical and polemical account of what could be called in the broadest sense Nietzsche's *economic philosophy*, that is his understanding of value, valuation, revaluation, and allied concepts. It is well known that Heidegger sees this entire dimension of Nietzsche's thought as the tragic fulfilment of Western metaphysics. As he says toward the end of the *Introduction to Metaphysics*:

> What seems more plausible than to take Plato's ideas in the sense of values and to interpret the being of *das seiende* from the standpoint of value?...
>
> *At bottom* this being [of values] meant neither more nor less than the presence of something already there, though not in so vulgar and handy a sense as tables and chairs...
>
> How stubbornly the idea of values ingrained itself in the nineteenth century can be seen from the fact that even Nietzsche, and precisely he, never departed from this perspective.... His entanglement in the thicket of the idea of values, his failure to understand its questionable origin, is the reason why Nietzsche did not attain to the true center of philosophy.[19]

In his lectures on Nietzsche Heidegger tells us that it was Nietzsche who put the word value "into circulation." As Heidegger would no doubt agree, the claim that the word could be put "into circulation" presupposes that there already was a functioning economy of exchange in which the value of key words and ideas can rise and fall. In putting the word into circulation Nietzsche would simply have been articulating part of the complex of modern ideas, as Heidegger suggests with respect to other aspects of his thought.[20]

Now the burden of Heidegger's polemic against thinking in terms of values is fairly clear: values, like the will to power, are one more expression of the demand for presence that has constituted the *hybris* of philosophy since Plato. In his Nietzsche book, Heidegger's most extended discussion of values and transvaluation takes place in the section called "European Nihilism." Here, as throughout most of the lectures, Heidegger accords a priority to Nietzsche's notes of 1887–1888, and comments at length on a few that appear in *The Will to Power*. He devotes several chapters to the analysis of a rather long note, number 12, from *The Will to Power* entitled "Decline of the Cosmological Values." Heidegger prepares the choice and discussion of this fragment by a complex strategy in which he specifies a number of criteria that must be fulfilled by a fragment on nihilism that would reward analysis. Such choice is important, for without it, he observes, "we would merely be surrendering ourselves to the pointless confusion of the editor's textual arrangement."[21] *After* the analysis of the fragment and the development of the polemic against valuational thinking, Heidegger mentions another wrongheaded approach to reading Nietzsche on the question of value that was followed by academic philosophers who produced philosophies and phenomenologies of value. For these misguided scholars

> Values themselves appeared to be things in themselves, which one might arrange into "systems." Although tacitly rejecting Nietzsche's philosophy, one rummaged through Nietzsche's writings, especially *Zarathustra*, for such values. Then, "more scientifically" than the "unscientific philosopher-poet" Nietzsche, one organized them into an "ethics of value."[22]

So Heidegger wants to situate his own reading between the false economy of a scientific, systematic study of values that takes them as presences and the arbitrary, disordered, and therefore wasteful activity of simply reading through the fragments of *The Will to Power* in the editors' order. That those fragments are Nietzsche's own excess and waste, many of which he had consigned to the garbage, adds a certain piquancy to Heidegger's concern for sound, fundamental principles of good business and efficient housekeeping.

The fragment itself, number 12, begins in its first long part by identifying three factors that contribute to the development of what Nietzsche calls *nihilism as a psychological state*. The first of these considerations is introduced as follows: "Nihilism, then, is the recognition of the long *squandering* (*Vergeudung*) of strength, the agony of the 'in vain,' the insecurity, the lack of any opportunity to recuperate and to regain tranquillity—being ashamed of oneself, as if one had *deceived* oneself all too long." Nietzsche says that one form of nihilism arises when human beings see that they have *squandered* themselves in such ways that recuperation no longer is possible. That is, it has been supposed that becoming has a goal, and that human actions have specific goals, which may contribute to the larger ones. But "now one grasps the fact that becoming aims at *nothing* and achieves *nothing*." It's the way the reader of Nietzsche might feel after years of poring over the published works, the *Nachlass*, the letters, and the personal testimony, only to discover that there was no final insight here, no central concept, no totalistic system, no perspective of all perspectives. One would feel that time, eyesight, money, and intellectual energy had been *squandered*. Now in discussing the fragment, Heidegger acutely distinguishes many of the uses of "value" and its derivatives and affiliates. He succeeds in articulating the way this notion *circulates* in Nietzsche's text. But he has nothing to say about *squandering* as such, even though Nietzsche emphasizes the word and says that its recognition is the first occasion of a certain sort of nihilism—the process by which the highest values devalue themselves and which is the necessary presupposition of an *Umwertung aller Werthe*. We may be reminded here of that absence of commentary, documented in Derrida's *Spurs*, on the phrase *sie wird Weib* in Heidegger's performance of *Twilight of the Idols*. Perhaps there is some relation between squandering and becoming woman that would lead to their neglect in Heidegger's bravura close readings.

Squandering, as we have seen already, is thematized in *Zarathustra*'s economic discourse. To the men in the marketplace Zarathustra says "I love him whose soul squanders itself, who wants no thanks and returns none; for he always gives away and does not want to preserve himself." And at the beginning of the fourth part he describes himself as a squanderer. Having just deceived his animals with the ruse that he is going off to perform the honey sacrifice, he asks: "Why sacrifice? I squander what is given to me, I a squanderer with a thousand hands: how could I call that sacrificing?" (Z, 252, 4, 296). Later we will have to give some attention to the distinction among different forms of loss and surrender, such as is marked here between sacrifice (*Opfern*) and squandering. Presumably sacrifice, because it is regular and institutional, relies on and reinforces an ethos of regulated exchange—if not between men and gods then between men and the earth or within the social structure itself. Clearly squandering (*Verschwenden* or *Vergeudung*) has at least a double value in Nietzsche's texts. From the nihilistic standpoint analyzed in *The Will to Power*, 12, squandering is seen as a loss that weakens and exhausts the agent; the recognition of that waste leads to the belief that everything is in vain. Yet Zarathustra's uses of *Verschwenden* and similar terms suggest the Dionysian joy in destruction, expenditure, and *dépense* that inspired Bataille.

Heidegger does not consider the possibility that a transvaluation of values might also involve rethinking the associations of squandering. Yet, although he omits any discussion of this notion, he is careful to emphasize Nietzsche's use of an economic language in the fragment analyzed, especially such terms as *invest* and *withdraw* so that Nietzsche's account of how values are attributed to things and then denied of them begins to sound like the buying and selling of stocks. The bottom line of Heidegger's reading of the fragment on nihilism and Nietzsche's general understanding of nihilism is that that understanding itself is nihilistic because it arises from "valuative thought" (*Wertgedanken*).[23] Yet Heidegger's reading is forced and narrow. In the fragment in question Nietzsche never com-

mits himself to a discourse of value *except* insofar as he is repro-
ducing the point of view of nihilism. It is nihilism for which the
world finally "seems *valueless*" after the invested values have
been withdrawn. It is "nihilism as a psychological state" that
Nietzsche aims at explicating; and to do so he impersonates the
nihilist who reckons up his profits and losses. Should we then
conclude the following with Heidegger?

> There are "results" only where there is reckoning and cal-
> culation. In fact Nietzsche's train of thought, as nihilistic, is
> reckoning (*Rechnen*).... To reckon psychologically means to
> appraise everything on the basis of value and to calculate
> value on the basis of the fundamental value, will to
> power—to figure how and to what extent "values" can be
> evaluated in accord with will to power and so prove valid.[24]

And Heidegger goes on to claim that "the will to power is the
object and the subject of a metaphysics thoroughly dominated
by valuative thinking."[25] In line with such a reading Heidegger
places the greatest weight on such phrases as "Principles of a
New Valuation" that appear in Nietzsche's notebooks; and he
understands the project of transvaluation as essentially a reversal of the hierarchy of values, rather than construing it (as one
might) as a transformation of valuative thinking.

I already have suggested that the circulation of gifts, symbolic exchange, expenditure, and squandering appear in
Zarathustra in such a way as to put in question Heidegger's
metaphysical reading of Nietzsche's economics. Yet it might be
said that the poetic mode of Nietzsche's "greatest gift" lends
itself to an archaicizing tendency in which scraps and memories
of premonetary cultures are introduced as part of the fantasmat-
ic time and place of Zarathustra's speeches. Consider then some
of the earliest and most fundamental themes of *Beyond Good and
Evil*, which Nietzsche describes as the no-saying companion
piece to *Zarathustra*. The first chapter is entitled "Of the Prejudices of Philosophers." It is true that Nietzsche opens that chapter by asking what the *value* of truth is, but he immediately
demonstrates that such a question must be uncanny in every
respect; to take it seriously is to call each of its terms into ques-

tion. It is an abyssal question, so that once thoughtfully asked we are at a loss to say "Which of us is Oedipus here? Which is the Sphinx?" (*BGE*, 1). One asks about the value of truth here not because value is the last word, retaining its meaning (its value) throughout the uncanny experience of questioning, but because it is a first word, a strategic way of unsettling the unreflective position that truth is of unquestioned value, that we know the value of truth and the truth of value. In the next section Nietzsche claims that "The fundamental belief of metaphysicians is the belief in opposite values" (*BGE*, 2). The true and the false, the real and the apparent, being and becoming—these binary distinctions and more are interrogated and deconstructed in the text that follows. It is not only the belief in "opposites" that is in question, however, but that in "opposite *values*. " Nietzsche then would be questioning the principle according to which, for example, if the value of reality rose the value of appearance would have to fall. But he also is questioning whether the opposition reality/appearance is a helpful or illuminating way of thinking. And, finally, he also may be asking whether there is some other form of value thinking, free of the metaphysical prejudice of opposite values. I suggest that his most coherent and perspicuous strategy is one that would either put the concept of value in question (for what are values that do not admit of opposites?) or that would lead to rethinking it in such a way that it would be radically different from our customary conception of value (for one thing, Nietzsche implies that this would be a nonmetaphysical conception of value). In part of his sermon on *die schenkende Tugend* Zarathustra says "Truly such a bestowing love must become a robber of all values" ("*Wahrlich, zum Rauber an allen Werthen muss solche schenkende Liebe werden*"). Values then are not the sorts of things that remain constant, in place, or present; the gift-giving virtue can seize and transform them. This is not a discourse of values but an injunction against the primacy of values.

To assess the place of values and valuations in *Zarathustra* it will be necessary to see them within a context in which squandering, allied to the gift-giving virtue, is not rejected but embraced. It is transvalued. In one sense Heidegger is right in warning us against constructing a "scientific" system of values

by rummaging around in *Thus Spoke Zarathustra*. We can antici-
pate that such systems will have difficulties comprehending the
praise of squandering. Although Heidegger does not name
these systematizers of value, we could think of Nicolai Hartmann's *Ethics*, published in 1926, which does indeed offer a
systematic account of the realm of values. And Hartmann
could plausibly be accused of having "rummaged" in *Thus
Spoke Zarathustra* for some of these values. For he calls one of
his three "self-sufficient virtues" *die schenkende Tugend*,
acknowledging that it was without a name until Nietzsche
attempted to define it.[26] However, Hartmann does not explore
the uncanny dimension of that baptism which Nietzsche
described as "naming the unnameable." For Hartmann *die
schenkende Tugend* has to do with what he calls *spiritual gifts;* the
law of giving and taking that pertains to such gifts is distinct
from that which governs material goods, for whoever bestows
such gifts is in no way diminished by them. *Radiant virtue* in
the English translation has a tendency to steer us away from
the ambivalence of the gift. Hartmann sees *die schenkende
Tugend* as a vast overflowing, a scattering of seeds broadcast
(he cites the parable of the sower). Everything about this virtue
is admirable and positive; the man who exemplifies it glows
like the sun. In the presence of those with this creative genius
"all hearts are opened. No one goes away from them except
laden with gifts, yet no one can say what he has received."[27]
Hartmann enthusiastically endorses Nietzsche's figure of the
sun and his praise of uselessness. Yet there is no hint of the
ambivalence that one finds in Nietzsche (or in Emerson, for
that matter!) in this analysis. Hartmann speaks of this virtue as
a "virtue without sacrifice," because "the imparter simply over-
flows."[28] Zarathustra, however, had told his disciples that they
desired to be sacrifices, to spend themselves. And although
Hartmann repeats the images of dissemination found in
Zarathustra (such virtue is like "wind-scattered pollen") he
omits any reference to episodes like "The Night Song" in which
the giver confesses his limits and his envy of those who
receive.[29] And Hartmann, who devotes much laborious inquiry
into the question of what laws of connection or order of priori-
ties might obtain among the many values of his phenomeno-

logical ethics, does not seem to have taken seriously Zarathustra's claim that *die schenkende Tugend* is first in the order of rank or, to put it in another fashion, that virtue precedes value. Nor does he have a place for Zarathustra's declarations that *die schenkende Tugend* is a robber of all values and identical with the lust to rule.

We can understand Heidegger's dismissing such procedures and sympathize with his turning to Nietzsche himself, who put the idea of value "into circulation." At the same time we must note the determined way in which Heidegger seeks to show a line of descent from Nietzschean value thinking to quasi-scientific theories of value or, worse, various thoughtless forms of value relativism.

We also wish that Heidegger's exploration of the sense of *es gibt* could have been enriched by a considerations of the giving and receiving, squandering and sacrificing, spending and expending in *Zarathustra*. Presumably Heidegger would include Nietzsche among those he accuses of a naive understanding, a thoughtless use of language in *es gibt*. No one in the Plato to Nietzsche tradition, Heidegger suggests, has heard the *gift* and the *giving* in *the given*. The charge would seem to hold against the dominant tendencies in English language philosophy, although we might want to note some countervailing currents in eccentrics like Emerson and Thoreau (whose *Walden* begins with a long chapter on "Economy"). The Heideggerian account of *es gibt* is bound up with his diagnosis of the metaphysics of presence. Perhaps that metaphysics already is inscribed in our language when we speak of *presenting* something to someone, of making her a *present*. The given, we suppose, is present, just as the gift is a present. Heidegger warned against such a reading of his own *es gibt*. In *Being and Time* he had written "Only so long as Dasein is, is there [*gibt es*] Being."[30] In the *Letter on Humanism* there is this clarification: "To be sure. It means that only so long as the lighting of Being comes to pass does Being convey itself to man. But the fact that the *Da*, the lighting as the truth of Being itself, comes to pass is the dispensation of Being itself.... The sentence does not say that Being is the product of man."[31] That is, it does not say that man produces the presence of Being, as if through the presence of his consciousness.

Heidegger would like us to listen to his language, to take what he has given us in the appropriate way, to be sensitive to his gift. Yet (as Heidegger also knows) to attend to the speaking of language would be to realize that when something is given there is always the possibility that something is held back, and the gift that is sent may always fail to reach the one for whom it is destined. If there is giving, there is also receiving; gifts may be gratefully acknowledged, accepted only with reservations as the workings of a dominating power, or rejected and scorned by an evil, envious eye. Nietzsche indicates all of these possibilities by means of the complex protocols that accompany the presentation of the great gift of *Zarathustra*. And he does not fail to make use of the possibilities of this sort lurking in the German language in which *Gabe* can be either a gift or a dose and in which *Gift*, which now means poison once had the sense of our English *gift* or *present*. In this light we might read one of Nietzsche's notes from the period of *Zarathustra's* composition: *"'Es gibt sich': sagt eure Bequemlichkeit" Nein, es nimmt sich und wird immer sich nehmen"* ("Does your laziness say 'It gives itself?' No, it is taken and it will always be taken") (10, 497). Here Nietzsche seems to respond to the same metaphysical and linguistic naivete that Heidegger identifies. And he suggests not only that we should hear the giving in the given but that along with the giving there also must be a taking. There is a play of giving and receiving, of presenting and withholding, of presence and absence. In *Zarathustra* this note is taken up and transformed within one of the speeches "Of the Virtue That Makes Small":

> *"Es gibt sich"—das ist auch eine Lehre von Ergebung. Aber ich sage euch, ihr Behaglichen: es nimmt sich und wird immer mehr noch von euch nehmen!*
>
> "It is given"—that is also a doctrine of submission. But I tell you, you comfortable people: *it is taken*, and will be taken more and more from you!

The two forms of the saying vary from the more general, one might say the ontological, to the economic and the hortatory. In German *es gibt sich* suggests a certain confidence or expectation, a reliance that things will continue to be given. This is a tone that also can be found in many of Heidegger's discussions of the *es gibt*. Comfort and assurance must be placed in an economy in which their fragility becomes obvious. The "present" is nothing but a moment in such an economy; Nietzsche's coinage *es nimmt sich* is a criticism of the metaphysics of presence *avant la lettre*.

Jacques Derrida has already pointed to the obliquity in Heidegger's reading of Nietzsche that circles around property and the gift. In *Spurs* he says

> it is not from an onto-phenomenological or semantico-hermeneutic interrogation that property (*propre*) is to be derived. For the question of the truth of being is not *capable* of the question of property. On the contrary, it falls short of the undecidable exchange of more into less.[32]

And Derrida warns us that we ought not to dispense with "the critical resources of the ontological question" as raised by Heidegger to assume that we *know* what property and all of its affiliates are: "propriation, exchange, give, take, debit, price, etc." These are significant remarks for the reading of *Zarathustra*, to the extent that these very words and thoughts are thematized and problematized there. On one level this text with its talk of gift giving, revenge, envy, squandering, and sacrifice may appear to take place on a precritical level in which many of the contents of a preindustrial folk psychology seem to have been incorporated into a poetic production. Yet if we listen to Derrida's warning not to assume that we know what such contents are, we might be open to a reading of Nietzsche that is more responsive to his dangerous and risky gift. Incidentally, it may be worth noting that Mauss had in his way, and at a lesser level of generality, said something similar in his *Essay on the Gift*, fifty years before Derrida's *Spurs*. The latter statement—a truly Socratic confession of ignorance—says of the structuralist investigations of recent years what Mauss had said of positivist ethnography and ethnocentric popular views of social practices. Namely, they assume too much, thinking that the laws of property are accessible to us when we hardly know what property is. If these warnings are right, then it may be said that we have hardly begun to read *Thus Spoke Zarathustra* if we do not know what gifts are—gifts, for example such as the one that Zarathustra was carrying down the mountain, the present passed to him in secret by the little old woman, or the gift that Nietzsche addressed to humanity. These *presents* are as difficult for us to understand as *presence* itself, and for much the same reasons.

Notes

1. Although Harold Alderman has entitled his book on Nietzsche, devoted mainly to *Thus Spoke Zarathustra*, *Nietzsche's Gift*, he does not thematize the subject of the title.

2. Marcel Mauss, *The Gift: Forms and Functions of Exchange in Archaic Societies*, trans. L. Cunnison (New York, 1967), pp. 31, 70.

3. Ibid., p. 72.

4. See Jacques Derrida, *Spurs/Éperons*, trans. Barbara Harlow (Chicago, 1979), p. 121.

5. Responses to and amplification of Mauss's work include the following. Emile Benveniste, "Gift and Exchange in the Indo-European vocabulary," in *Problems in General Linguistics*, trans. Mary Elizabeth Meek (Coral Gables, Fla., 1971), pp. 271–280; Georges Bataille, "The Notion of Expenditure" and "Sacrifices" in *Visions of Excess*, ed. Allan Stoekl (Minneapolis, 1985); Claude Lévi-Strauss "Introduction a l'oeuvre de Marcel Mauss," in Marcel Mauss, *Sociologie et anthropologie* (Paris, 1950), pp. ix–lii; Maurice Merleau-Ponty, "From Mauss to Lévi-Strauss," in *Signs* (Evanston, 1964); Rodolphe Gasché, "L'Échange heliocentrique" in *L'Arc*, no. 48 (1972): 73–84; Marshall Sahlins, "The Spirit of the Gift," in *Stone Age Economics* (New York, 1972). Some of Jean Baudrillard's writing is also relevant; see especially "When Bataille Attacked the Metaphysical Principle of Economy," *Canadian Journal of Political and Social Theory* 11, no. 3 (Fall 1987): 57–62; and *The Mirror of Production*, trans. Mark Poster (St. Louis, 1975).

6. On the concept of envy and the evil eye, see my "Nietzsche on Envy," *International Studies in Philosophy* (1983): 269–276.

7. Ralph Waldo Emerson, "Gifts" in *Essays and Lectures* (New York, 1983), p. 536.

8. Ibid., p. 537.

9. This same notebook page (*10*, 512) contains a citation from Emerson that Nietzsche employs to sketch Zarathustra's posing of the question, "Who are my friends?"

10. Nietzsche *Werke*, ed. Musarion, vol. 9, p. 238 (cited by Walter Kaufmann, "Translator's Introduction" to *The Gay Science*, pp. 11–12).

11. Emerson, "Politics," in *Essays and Lectures*, pp. 567–568.

12. Ibid., p. 535.

13. Ibid., p. 300. On Emerson's economic thought, see Richard A. Grusin. "'Put God in Your Debt': Emerson's Economy of Expenditure," *PMLA* (January 1988): 35–44. Discussions of Nietzsche's reading of and use of Emerson are to be found in Edward Baumgarten, *Das Vorbild Emersons in Werk and Leben Nietzsches* (Heidelberg, 1957); Stanley Hubbard, *Nietzsche und Emerson* (Basel, 1958); Walter Kaufmann, trans., *The Gay Science* (New York, 1974) "Translator's Introduction," pp. 7–13.

14. In "Gifts," Emerson writes: "It is a very onerous business, this of being served, and the debtor naturally wishes to give you a slap. A golden text for these gentlemen is that which I so admire in the Buddhist who never thanks, and who says, 'Do not flatter your benefactors'" (*Essays and Lectures*, p. 532).

15. Cf. also my discussion of the metaphorics of this chapter in *Nietzschean Narrative* (Bloomington, Ind., 1989), pp. 53–59.

16. David Farrell Krell, *Postponements* (Bloomington, Ind., 1986).

17. Michael Serres, *The Parasite*, trans. Lawrence R. Schehr (Baltimore, 1982), pp. 225, 227.

18. Rodolphe Gasché offers a suggestive analysis of some of the tensions and dualities in Mauss's conception of the gift in "L'Échange heliocentrique," Gasché articulates Mauss's project of identifying an object for the social sciences (the practice of exchange), which would be transparent and self-identical. This leads him to construct a theory of the gift according to which the system of "total prestations" is harmonious and essentially circular, in the image of the sun as the guarantor and chief example of cosmic order. The consequence is to reduce expenditive or *dépense* to an effect or atmosphere that will be explained by the laws of circulation, to minimize the significance of agonistic exchange, to enforce a certain conception of property and self-identity through the view that all gifts eventually come back to the giver (and so function as means of what we might call Hegelian

reappropriation of the self) and to reduce the differences (which on another level Mauss would like to emphasize) between archaic societies and our own, by describing both as subject to laws of closed circulation. In contrast Georges Bataille suggests the possibility, as Gasché points out, of a more radical conception of expenditure in which the sun functions as giving to excess, without return. Marshall Sahlins comes to a similar view of Mauss that emphasizes the surprising affinities between his conception of "total prestation" and modern social contract theory; cf. Sahlins, "The Spirit of the Gift."

19. Martin Heidegger, *An Introduction to Metaphysics*, trans. Ralph Manheim (New York, 1961), p. 167.

20. Martin Heidegger, *Nietzsche, Volume IV: Nihilism*, trans. Frank A. Capuzzi and ed. David Farrell Krell (New York, 1982), pp. 16–17.

21. Ibid., p. 13.

22. Ibid., p. 59.

23. Ibid., p. 22.

24. Ibid., p. 48.

25. Ibid., p. 53.

26. Nicolai Hartmann, *Ethics, Volume II: Moral Values*, trans. Stanton Coit (New York, 1932), pp. 332–340.

27. Ibid., p. 336.

28. Ibid., pp. 334–335.

29. Ibid., p. 338.

30. Martin Heidegger, *Sein und Zeit* (Tübingen, 1984), p. 212.

31. Martin Heidegger, *Basic Writings*, ed. David Farrell Krell (New York, 1977), p. 216.

32. Derrida, *Spurs*, pp. 111, 113.

Parasites and Their Noise

It would be a mistake to imagine that it is possible merely by a vigorous shout to frighten away such a playful thing as the opera, as if it were a specter. He who would destroy the opera must take up the struggle against Alexandrian cheerfulness, which expresses itself so naively in opera concerning its favorite idea.... By what sap is this parasitic opera nourished, if not by that of true art?

—*The Birth of Tragedy*, 19; 1, 125–126

What is it that Nietzsche gives when he gives *Zarathustra* to humanity? The recipients often have been in a quarrelsome mood about this "greatest present" and have tended to argue that Nietzsche does not really give enough, that he holds something back, or that he gives too much, running to excess and spoiling the integrity of his gift. Not enough, this is the characterization of the book by those who think that it is suggestive but not articulate, that it hints but does not reason and argue. Too much, the claim here is that Nietzsche is repetitious and bombastic, inundating us with an excessive overflow of images and anecdotes. Heidegger, who finds the best statement of Nietzsche's philosophy in the notes of his last two years, presumably holds *Zarathustra* to be incomplete, a tentative approach to the doctrine of the will to power. Nietzsche never quite managed to give us the gift he intended (one that turns out to be what the metaphysical tradition has been trying to

give us all along), so we have to help him out. That strategy
could be seen as entailing the advantage that we simultaneously receive a gift and pay back the debt we incur; we refuse the
position of the parasite who would simply be overwhelmed by
the power of the great thinker. "One repays a teacher badly if
one remains only a pupil" (Z, 103; 4, 101). But perhaps (and this
may be another way of avoiding the debt) Nietzsche's gift may
not be in the best of taste? Perhaps he adds too much and does
not know where to stop?

The most frequently discussed breach of taste is Part IV of
Zarathustra. That is Eugen Fink's view: he describes this last
part of our *Zarathustra* as a "sudden crash (*Absturz*)," in which
Nietzsche ceases to philosophize and instead seeks to "create
an image of existence."[1] In a book devoted to *Thus Spoke
Zarathustra*, Lawrence Lampert seems to agree that Part IV is a
supplement and a parasitic growth on a poetically and philo-
sophically complete work. In *Nietzsche's Teaching* he relegates
the discussion of this part of the text to an appendix, "Part
IV—An Interlude between the Main Acts," which begins:

> It was fitting that Part IV of *Thus Spoke Zarathustra* be pri-
> vately printed and circulated secretly in only a handful of
> copies among Nietzsche's friends, for the existence of a
> fourth part violates the end of Part III. Everything points
> to the end of Part III as The End. It is, as the animals say,
> the end of Zarathustra's going under.[2]

So Lampert would like to distinguish the true whole of
Zarathustra from its accretions. Before even worrying about
such things as the notebooks that contain plans for fifth and
sixth parts, he will draw the line at the place between the public and the private. But how easily can such a line be drawn? It
is true that on the reverse side of the title page of *Zarathustra* IV
it says "For my friends and not for the public (*Für meine Freunde und nicht für die Öffentlichkeit*)." One might wonder about
the distribution to a few friends. In some hermeneutic orders, a
more esoteric communication of this sort would be regarded as
a possible key to the author's project, one that would cast light
on the more widely published parts.

Nietzsche also had something to say about friends and friendship and the sorts of exchange dictated by the relationship; Zarathustra speaks on these themes in the indisputably "authentic" parts of the gift, for example in "Of the Friend." So one might ask whether something done under the double sign of friendship and *Zarathustra* ought not to have some initial claim to be taken seriously and read perhaps with some attention to the question of friendship and its structures. What if friendship and the possibility of the exchanges it requires were themselves thematized not only in *Zarathustra* but especially in this "private communication to friends"? One might have to ask who Nietzsche's friends are, in what sense it is possible to be a friend, and in what sense is a "private" publication or communication really possible? In Nietzsche's letters that speak of Part IV, his correspondents are enjoined to the strictest secrecy concerning its existence. To von Gersdorff he says that the words *publicity* and *the public* (*Öffentlichkeit* and *Publikum*) sound to him "in relation to my whole *Zarathustra*, approximately like 'whorehouse' and 'public girl.'"[3] Nietzsche, however, wrote many people asking them to keep his secret, like someone confiding an amorous adventure to too many friends and swearing each to secrecy. At first he wanted twenty copies printed, but then abruptly doubled his requisition. As soon as he began to distribute the copies, he became nervous about whether the postal system had let them fall into the wrong hands, recognizing, so it seems, that all letters and messages may fail to arrive at their destinations (although he continued to repeat that *Zarathustra will* find its proper readers centuries hence).[4] Once the forty copies were available Nietzsche further compromised his privacy by means of a complex system of postal instructions that included directives to Peter Gast to mail them out to the "friends." When all was said and done Nietzsche had sent copies to a Fräulein Druscowitz, apparently on the strength of a single letter she had written him, and to Fräulein Rohr, a mutual friend of his and Malwida von Meysenburg.[5] In December 1888, Nietzsche asked for Peter Gast's help in recovering all the copies of Part IV, confessing that he did not recall how many copies had been printed or to whom they had been sent.[6] Perhaps this was a "secret" designed, like so many, to excite public curiosity and interest; maybe Nietzsche hoped to whet the appetite of publishers and the public.

Writing to Carl Fuchs in July 1888, Nietzsche touches on the topic of friendship and privacy:

> In the meantime I have given instructions for one of the few copies of my *ineditum* to be sent to you, as a sign that all is well between us again and that the *farouche* moment of an all too vulnerable and all too solitary soul is past. The fourth part of *Zarathustra:* treated by me with that shyness vis-a-vis the public, which I bitterly regret not having shown in the case of the first three parts...[7]

One might conclude, then, that all of *Zarathustra* is essentially "private" (as Nietzsche expressed the wish that it were) or that none of it is (as he in fact distributed copies of Part IV, sometimes rather freely).

Let us return to the commentators and the facts to which they allude in support of a certain standard view of the text, a view that requires a closure and excludes the unnecessary, the excessive, and the supplementary. If the closure is not in what we think of as the standard text (for example, the four-part text as it appears in the Colli-Montinari edition), then some of the text must be excised. And in this case the facts of the work's publication and some of Nietzsche's own statements are brought forward to justify the excision, although it is odd to appeal to the authority of the animals (as Lampert does) to justify the excision, especially considering the prominent role that animals and animallike behavior play in Part IV. Before we can draw conclusions from what the animals say, we need to know what it means when animals speak. One might wonder why not only higher men come to Zarathustra's cave as (perhaps) candidates for friendship, but also a full array of animals (his eagle and snake, the ass brought by the kings, the cows to whom the Voluntary Beggar preaches, the laughing lion and the flock of doves, and then all the animals evoked in song). Nietzsche said that *Zarathustra* could not be understood properly unless one heard its "halcyon tone"; but, as we shall see, in one significant line of interpretation, the halcyon tone is the song of a bird. Could a philosophical bestiary play some role in articulating the space between animal and *Übermensch*, the space in which the higher men move and in which the question of friendship becomes acute? On January 18, 1884, Nietzsche writes to his publisher at that time, Ernst Schmeitzner, that *Zarathustra* is "ready," that the third part is the "conclusion" (*Schluss*) of the first two, and describes it as the "third act of my drama (or I should rather say the finale of my symphony)," expressions that he repeats in a number of letters to friends.[8] However, Nietzsche's statements take on a different tone once Part IV is written. He did circulate that section privately; but by then he had broken with Schmeitzner, the anti-Semitic publisher of Parts I–III and says that he is not going public with Part IV *both* because there is not yet an appropriate audience for it *and* because he no longer has a publisher.[9] Moreover, we might wonder just what Nietzsche was saying when he described Parts I–III as the completion of his "drama" or his "symphony." These, speaking loosely, are metaphorical descriptions of the kind of text in question. *Zarathustra* I–III might yet be incomplete as a philosophical or poetico-philosophical work or as a personal confession or as a venture in a new kind of thinking. As far back as November 1883 (before *Zarathustra* III had been completed), Nietzsche wrote to Overbeck that the book had four parts, had to be evaluated as a whole, and was the furthest thing from "literature."[10] By February 1885, Part IV itself had taken on the title of the finale, even the "sublime finale" in Nietzsche's letters to those friends to whom he would eventually distribute it.[11] And in May 1885 he was explicit in telling Overbeck "It is intended as a finale: just read once more the 'Preface' to the first part."[12]

To read Nietzsche seriously (which includes the possibility of comic readings) would seem at the very least to involve problematizing the conceptions of completeness and authorial intention that lead readers (not only of Nietzsche's works) to constitute canons that include some texts and exclude others. The literary remains hardly point to a single, unequivocal view. The notebooks contained sketches and plans for fifth and sixth parts of *Zarathustra* that he continued to contemplate for a year or so after writing Part IV. David Krell has performed a remark-

able job of reading in arguing that all of *Zarathustra* as we have
it can be seen as a determined series of evasions or postponements of Zarathustra's (and Nietzsche's) confrontation with
woman, death, and sensuality.[13] Zarathustra asked himself in
"The Stillest Hour" why he was still deferring his most significant task, a task that involved his own *Untergehen* and a connection with his children. Even the signs (*Zeichen*) of the doves
and the laughing lion that appear at the end of Part IV could
seem to be postponements of that confrontation; at most they
are pointers to other signs or events that are clearly never manifest in the story as we have it. Given Krell's reading, we might
hear a note of desperation both in Nietzsche's repeated assur-
ances in 1884 that Part III is the finale of his symphony and in
his later notes where he says that Part IV will be the fulfillment
of the *Vorrede*. Later I will want to say something about what
sort of fulfillment that might be.

Clearly it would be possible to multiply such philological
and hermeneutic complexities indefinitely. For example, in *Ecce
Homo* Nietzsche alludes to the fourth part of *Zarathustra* (*EH*,
228; *6*, 270–271). Should we then regard *Ecce Homo* as the last
authoritative statement and conclude from this allusion that
Zarathustra IV belongs to the whole? Such a proceeding would
be foreclosed by the fact that in the same work Nietzsche
speaks of being finished with *Zarathustra* when he completed
Part III. Part IV then, from the standpoint of this "last will and
testament," would be both inside and outside of *Thus Spoke
Zarathustra*. Yet perhaps interpretations ought not to be multi-
plied without necessity. Let me suggest, however, that most
readings of *Zarathustra* IV, whether they see it as a completely
unfortunate afterthought or as the satyr play that provides
relief and tonic modulation from the heavier tones of what precedes it, agree in describing it as parasitic on Nietzsche's essential text.[14] But Nietzsche himself has something to say about
parasites and parasitism. In section 19 of "On Old and New
Tablets," Zarathustra describes the parasite (*Schmarotzer*) as
something that necessarily attaches itself to the highest soul.
And, as we soon shall see, the higher men who seek Zarathustra in Part IV, whether to celebrate him and attempt to live off
his strength or, like the *Zauberer*, to attack him out of envy,

exemplify various species of parasites. Could it be that readings of *Zarathustra* IV that denounce or categorize it as parasitic on an essential text are refractions at some odd angle of Nietzsche's own attempt to articulate something of the logic of parasitism? Parasitism can characterize all of these: the strange assortment of types that express their cry of need in Zarathustra's kingdom, the ways in which one text is related to others, the relations that readers have to texts, and the affiliations that readings have with other readings.

Parasites of many sorts turn up in Nietzsche's notes, those notes that are either parasitic on the published texts or that, as Heidegger would have it, point toward a genuine Nietzschean philosophy on which the published texts feast parasitically, obscuring the true shape, the meat, the organic integrity of the doctrines. Already in the fall of 1883, Nietzsche made plans for a fourth part of Zarathustra, according to the following outline (I quote the first few lines):

> The king and the fool have an idea that Zarathustra's coming is *necessary*.
>
> Zarathustra closes ever narrower circles: great speeches, in which he *excludes*. Ever smaller circles on higher mountains.
>
> At first (1) the parasites are excluded, then (2) the hypocrites (3) the weak who are of good will, then (4) the unconscious hypocrites of morality. (*10,* 593)

Can the parasites be excluded so easily at the beginning? Or should we suspect that all who cry out in desperation, winning for themselves an invitation to eat and drink at Zarathustra's cave, protected by his animals, are parasites? Can we identify the parasite and the parasite relationship in terms of who feeds off whom? By that standard all of Zarathustra's guests are parasites and he plays the host, a host rich and strong enough to maintain a diverse and noisy brood of parasites.

Why investigate parasitism, why attempt to articulate its structure? Nietzsche, it seems, has already parodied such an interest in his presentation of the figure of the Conscientious Man of the Spirit (*der Gewissenhafte des Geistes*). Zarathustra stumbles over him accidentally on his way to answer the cry of distress. The Conscientious Man has his head in the muck because he is conscientiously studying a parasite, the leech (*Blutegel*), more specifically, the brain of the leech. Now he not only studies the leech with all scientific dedication and rigor, he does so by becoming the leech's host allowing it (or *them*—parasites always come in multiples) to parasite his own body. That he studies the *brain* of the leech suggests that he wants to understand how parasitism works, to uncover its mental laws. But his study of parasitism is reductive and limited. He stops here, rather than going on to consider other animal parasites or the possibility that parasitism might be a general phenomenon in the world of men. Like the other higher men his thoughts are parasitic on those of Zarathustra, so that he is the middle link in a chain of parasitic relations, Zarathustra's parasite, parasited by leeches. He explains himself by proudly quoting Zarathustra's own words back to him:

> "Because you, O Zarathustra, once said 'Spirit is the life that itself cuts into life,' that introduced me and seduced me to your doctrine. And truly with my own blood have I increased my own knowledge."
>
> "As the evidence indicates," Zarathustra interposed, for the blood continued to flow down the naked arm of the man of conscience, for ten leeches had bitten into it. (Z, 264; 4, 321)

But we should not suppose, because of this scientist's reductive understanding of Zarathustra's teaching, that the subject matter of his study, properly understood, is not a significant concern. In extending his invitation to the Conscientious Man, Zarathustra thanks him for what he has learned from him. But what did he learn? Might Zarathustra have observed that one organism's parasite is another's host? That is, the structure has a perfectly general nature although Zarathustra hesitates, as he says, to "pour all [that he has learned] into the strict ears" of the bleeding man. Some ears are more open than others; some do not know that what is noise and interruption in one context becomes crucial and even musical in another.

What they learn exhibits the difference between this field biologist of the spirit and Zarathustra. The Conscientious Man, as his later conversations also show, is committed to the most intensive and rigorous study of a limited and tightly defined domain of the real, whereas Zarathustra observes and acts on relations and structures in their generality. He is a structuralist, we might say, whereas the Conscientious Man is a positivist. Ought the generality to be extended in the way that the student of the leech suggests, perhaps unconsciously, when he calls Zarathustra the "great leech of the conscience"? Is Zarathustra a medicinal parasite, one who relieves the conscientious of their excesses and restores them to a dryer, healthier state? (At the same time, let us remember, Zarathustra is putting himself into the position of host when he invites the Conscientious Man to his cave.) Is there then no parasite *an sich* but only a parasitic relation that would have to be investigated by methods quite different from the positivistic fetishism involved in devoting one's life to the brain of the leech? Note that the latter project involves a reversal so that one becomes dependent on one's dependent, the parasite of one's parasite. Certainly this would constitute a modification of what Zarathustra had said about parasites in "On Old and New Tablets," which may now be worth reading at some length:

> wherever you would climb with me, O my brothers, see to it that no *parasite* climbs with you. Parasite: that is a worm, a creeping, supple worm that wants to grow fat on your sick sore places.... Where the strong man is weak, when the noble man is too gentle, there it builds its nauseating nest (*ekles Nest*)...
> Which is the highest type of being and which the lowest? The parasite is the lowest type; but he who is of the highest type nourishes the most parasites.
> For the soul which possesses the longest ladder and can descend the deepest; how should the most parasites not sit upon it? (Z, 225; 4, 260–261)

If the parasite is something like a necessary accompaniment of the highest and deepest soul, then one may wonder how

Zarathustra can ask his "brothers" to leave all parasites behind when they climb with him. A parasite, it is said, has a nauseating nest (*ekles Nest*); in the very next chapter, "*Der Genesende, Zarathustra confronts nausea* (Ekel) when he is overcome by his abysmal thought. Everything about the parasite seems to be a function of its mouth: eating (including sucking, like the leech); noise making; and provoking nausea or vomiting. The abysmal thought is not the eternal recurrence as such but (as Zarathustra says) "the eternal recurrence even of the smallest—that was my disgust (*Überdruss*) with all existence. *Ach, Ekel, Ekel, Ekel*" (Z, 236; 4, 274–75).

We can read *Zarathustra* IV as an allegory of the parasite. If we do so we will not attend exclusively to individual speeches and thoughts but to the structure and motifs of the narrative, which still have not been fully explored. Consider some of the bare outline. The story begins with talk of food and squandering ("The Honey-Sacrifice") and reaches a culmination of sorts in the supper, party, and potlatch that Zarathustra provides for the higher men. Their collective cry of distress seduces Zarathustra to his final sin, pity—pity, we might add for the parasite. They all seek the stronger Zarathustra who will provide both their spiritual and intellectual victuals. Food, and the food chain, is of constant interest, ranging from the freely provided honey, to the wine brought by the two kings, to the voluntary beggar's attempt to opt out of the cycle of parasitism with a vegetarian diet. Everyone wants to be taken care of and Zarathustra is the universal host, providing food, shelter, and entertainment in the form of his long afterdinner talk on the higher men. He's such a good host that he gets the higher men to talking with and amusing one another to the point that they are able to carry on quite swimmingly when he leaves them, twice, to seek some relief from the hubbub. And these are noisy guests, parasites who make their presence known through squabbles, songs, and even by introducing the noisy ritual of the ass festival.

In French and the romance languages, *parasite* and its derivatives have the sense of static or noisy interference as well as the biological sense of a specific class of organisms that feed off but do not destroy others, and the social sense that applies to human beings who profit, similarly, from others. Following Michel Serres in *The Parasite* I want to demonstrate that Nietzsche saw these apparently diverse senses as part of a system.[15]

Parasites can be noisy; their noise is an aspect of their interference with and interruption of a system that, it seems, might go on its own quiet way without them. Perhaps they are like the parasitic mother and sister whom the philosopher called the greatest objection to his thought of eternal recurrence, who were constantly injecting themselves into his life, if only through noisy letters and sometimes, as in the Paul Rée–Lou Salomé –Nietzsche scandal, gnawing away at his innards and producing a great deal of commotion throughout the European postal system. Part IV contains the greatest variety of animals in *Zarathustra*, and these animals are introduced in their specificity and differentiation, not only in a generic opposition to the human. The leech, the cows, the ass, birds, the laughing lion, the lamb that is eaten, the dead snakes in the valley of snakes' death, the bees who provide the honey, Zarathustra's own animals (the eagle and serpent who gather food for everyone), the images of animals that appear in the songs of the *Zauberer* and the Shadow—these constitute a diversified array of the animal kingdom that is structured in part according to which animals or plants the various species eat and what or who eats them. This is a much more finely differentiated bestiary than one typically finds in philosophers; Heidegger, for example, uses a fairly simple opposition between beast and man and tends to use insects as his chief instance of animal life.[16] In the *Vorrede* the holy man had urged Zarathustra to become animal: "Do not go to men, but stay in the forest! Go rather to the animals! Why will you not be as I am—a bear among bears, a bird among birds?" (Z, 41; *4*, 13). And what does the holy man do in the forest? He sings, laughs, and weeps, that is he *resonates;* and among his sounds are animal noises for he says that part of his repertoire is *Brummen* ("growling"; said, for example, of a bear). In living alone the *Heilige* must provide his own music as he provides for all of his economic needs.[17] In the forest and mountain scenes of Part IV Zarathustra will be working out his relations to men by means of a complex set of relations of men to animals that will also be marked by a variety of voices and noises.

In some of his notes, Nietzsche suggests that Part IV is the fulfillment of the themes of the *Vorrede* of *Zarathustra*. How might we understand this in terms of the relations of guest and host, man and animal? In that preliminary series of episodes Zarathustra announces the subject of giving and receiving. He gives a series of speeches that elicit no intelligent response but which are continually interrupted. The crowd wants a spectacle, not a lecture, but the tightrope walker is displaced by the jester, the *Possenreisser* who is parasitic upon him, jumping into or over his place. With the death of the tightrope walker Zarathustra becomes a beggar and a supplicant rather than a giver. Having come down the mountain with a gift he is reduced to begging for food and drink in the middle of the night at an isolated house. And when he finds a host, he's told that not only he but the corpse too must eat and drink so as not to insult the laws of hospitality. There's a contrast here between the holy man (*der Heilige*) who aims at a closed economy by living from the roots that he has gathered and the hermit (*Einsiedler*) who insists on performing the culinary functions of the host, demanding that even the dead (the tightrope walker) accept his offering of food. Zarathustra has to deal first with an undervaluing then an over-valuing of hospitality. In the fourth part Zarathustra begins by announcing that he is a squanderer who has no need for the reg-ularities of sacrifice. It is a kind of intensification and parodic renewal of his first homage to the sun. He ends up entertaining not a live man and a corpse but eight higher men (men who are both dead and alive). In fact he provides a potlatch that over-whelms them and drives them to drunken excess. For the uncomprehending noise of the crowd in the marketplace, Part IV substitutes the noise of the higher men, a noise in his own cave and one that he can interrupt himself. Playing the host, Zarathustra demonstrates how the gift-giving virtue modulates into the lust to rule and how those who thoughtlessly affirm that "it gives itself" (even of Zarathustra and his teachings) will find that it is taken from them.

When *Thus Spoke Zarathustra* changes from being mainly a sequence of Zarathustra's speeches to a more conventional nar-rative or dramatic form, it does so around a determined group of themes: feasting, partying, noise, and song. A number of readers, including myself on another occasion, have noted that *Zarathustra* is parasitic upon a vast range of Western literature, from the Bible to Goethe. Literary precedents for the eating and drinking, the festivities, the inversion of religious ritual in the *Eselfest*, the competition of songs in which the parasites sing for their supper could be cited from Petronius, Rabelais, the fables of La Fontaine, certain episodes of Rousseau's *Confessions*, Diderot's *Rameau's Nephew*, and perhaps, above all, from Plato's *Symposium* or *Banquet*. This list, with the exception of Plato, is drawn from the Latin and romance languages that Germanic readers (one thinks especially of Heidegger here) have under-valued or ignored. And when only the apparently frivolous themes of such works are considered (neglecting their Platonic legitimation) one might be inclined to dismiss them as philo-sophically irrelevant in comparison with Sophocles and Hölderlin. But perhaps that dismissal is rather hasty, as would be the judgment declaring one language or literature to be merely parasitic on another without undertaking a vigilant inquiry into the nature of parasitism. And there are some exam-ples of such inquiries, notably Michel Serres's study of *The Par-asite* and Mikhail Bakhtin's *Rabelais and His World*. These stories of feasting typically exhibit complex structures that have to do with consumption, excess, open and closed systems, noise and interruptions.

Consider La Fontaine's fable of "The City Rat and the Country Rat" which Serres analyzes as a paradigm of such nar-ratives.[18] The city rat invites the country rat to dinner at the house where he is a parasite. They dine on the scraps and left-overs of the tax-farmer who owns the house; in other words, the country rat here is the parasite of a parasite of a parasite. But this feast, like so many others, is interrupted by a loud noise at the door. Enter the householder, the primary parasite of this series. For the rats, the interruption or noise of his arrival is an imposition and an obstacle; it threatens their dis-placement, so it seems, by one more parasite in the chain who would parasite them. Yet in this case, as we see, the source of the noise is identical in fact with the one who plays the host. He had been alerted by the gnawing and scuttling of the rats. What seems to be noise turns out to close the loop and contribute to the articulation of a rigorous structure susceptible of an equally rigorous analysis. The stories that may appear to be nothing but noise—La Fontaine's fables, the concluding part of the *Symposium* ushered in by the scandalous interruption of Alcibiades' entrance, these strange goings-on in Zarathustra's mountains and his cave, that Heidegger never mentions and that Fink dismisses—all of these admit of another kind of reading. Just now as I was writing that sentence the telephone rang and interrupted me. My typist had conscientiously found a certain disorder or noise in the draft of a paper, in the form of an addition that had not been marked clearly for insertion into a particular place in the manuscript. For her this strange supplement, like some of Nietzsche's notes, was a noisy intrusion into her work. For me, writing, the telephone call is also an interruption; those of a rigorous Heideggerian disposition will just not answer, but will stay on the solitary path of thinking whatever the distractions, waiting for a more significant call. But sometimes noise is more than merely noise.

Perhaps this is the time to speak of the noise that breaks into Zarathustra's solitude; that is, the story of Part IV. He has grown old on the mountain; his hair has turned white. He still is attended faithfully by the eagle and the serpent who seem to enjoy bringing him his food. Once, when he had to beg for food, back when he was carrying the corpse of the tightrope walker, the animals were absent. They appeared only at noon of the next day but from that point on they supply his meals, notably the "yellow and red berries, grapes, rose apples, fragrant herbs, and pine cones" that they lay beside the convalescent along with the two lambs that they have robbed from shepherds. Many of Zarathustra's interchanges with the animals involve food; finally those two will help to gather what is necessary for the feast in Part IV. Is it worth noting that there are no predators, no beasts of prey in *Zarathustra*? The closest we come to that is the eagle who, in a sense, is domesticated. In a glancing reference to Nietzsche, Serres speaks of "the philosopher who wrote on eagle and lamb," in the course of arguing that parasitism and not predation is the general case of human and animal relations, rather than the exception.[19] Certainly Nietzsche, in one of his voices glorifies the "blond beast" (the lion) and refuses to share the resentful moralism of the lambs who invent free will to differentiate themselves from the "evil" birds of prey. But in *Zarathustra* IV, although there are songs and fantasies of predators, notably the Enchanter's second song where he depicts the poet (that is, himself) as a healthy, lusty beast of prey, these are demonstrated to be illusions by the action of the story in which parasitism is rampant. Altogether Zarathustra and the animals form a cozy little economy with a minimalist social structure. When the eagle and the snake appear to him at the end of the *Vorrede* their harmony is emphasized, a harmony announced by a loud sound at noon (to be juxtaposed, in the "fulfillment" with a midnight song):

> he looked inquiringly into the sky—for he heard above him the sharp cry of a bird. And behold! An eagle was sweeping through the air in wide circles, and from it was hanging a serpent, not like a prey but like a friend: for it was coiled around the eagle's neck (Z, 52–53; 4, 27).

Not only can animals be "like" friends (although Nietzsche, perhaps scrupulously, refrains from calling them friends straight out) but that *these* animals can appear so is of interest. There is a considerable literary and iconographic tradition of representing the eagle and serpent as enemies, typically with the virtuous eagle depicted as triumphing over the wicked serpent.[20] To make eagle and serpent mutually dependent and symbiotic is to mute the suggestion that the eagle is a bird of prey. When this trio is all at home they not only supply one another's needs, they form a society that expresses itself by means of ritual, like the honey sacrifice. So now Zarathustra takes leave of the eagle and the serpent. He's not really going to perform the honey-sacrifice; he's going to "squander" while fishing for "colorful fish and crabs" in the abysmal human sea. He wants to gather and squander at the same time. He'll be a fisher of men; but the fish want a meal too, so he'll bait the hook. The fisherman is both a host and a parasite; offering food he in fact is living off the fish. He is not a beast of prey.[21] In developing this figure of himself as a "fisher of men" Zarathustra is doing more than parodying the Christian gospels. He's making it clear that his squandering will be to cast out food as widely as possible; in this trope the sacrificial offering becomes bait and the men become animals:

> Sacrifice—what? I squander what is given me, I, a squanderer with a thousand hands: how could I call that—a sacrifice!
>
> And when I desired honey, I desired only bait and sweet syrup and gum, which even growling bears (*Brummbaren*) and strange, sullen, wicked birds are greedy for (Z, 252; 4, 296).

Zarathustra's bait above all is his honey, both the ambrosial food that his animals have accumulated and the honey that runs in his veins, the liquid form of his happiness. Honey is fluid (but dense) and divisible without end. It's the perfect treat, an ideal dish like ice cream that can be handed around and is sure to excite general interest. Honey can be stored up, sometimes for a long time, but it also circulates. In contrast to his fastidious taste in food and his susceptibility to whatever might cause nausea, Zarathustra's description of his honey, or rather, the order that he places with the eagle and serpent has a lingering, caressing tone; it must be "yellow, white, fine, ice-cool golden honey in the comb" (Z, 252; 4, 296). It's connected with other things that overflow and are given away, like the wisdom of which Zarathustra began by saying

> I am weary of my wisdom (*ich bin meiner Weisheit überdrus- sig*), like a bee that has gathered too much honey; I need hands outstretched to take it.
>
> I should like to give it away and distribute it (*ver- schenken und austeilen*), until the wise among men have again become happy in their folly and the poor happy in their wealth (Z, 39; 4, 11).

It's the perfect gift. The wise will be happy in their folly, the poor with their wealth: doesn't this describe the higher men who become light, dancing and singing?

Honey also is gold, but a fluid gold, a gold that can be

spread around and constantly replenished. However, it is not the gold of the gold standard, whose fetishism Marx was describing at about the same time that Nietzsche was writing "Of the Gift-Giving Virtue." This gold circulates differently through the food chain and around the table. Here it is part of a complex network. It is produced by the bees, whose labor so often is a philosophical figure for production itself, a production that neither the philosophical tradition nor Nietzsche wants to examine more closely. It's gathered by the animals, prudently, one supposes, so as not to injure the bees; the supply must be allowed to renew itself. Then it is brought to Zarathustra, the master of the sacrifice and feast who will squander it, dispense it or use it for bait as he pleases. And here it's finally consumed by the higher men, those noisy sponging guests. Zarathustra is clear about the structure of this food chain:

> For although the world is like a dark animal jungle (*ein dunkler Thierwald*) and a pleasure-garden for all wild hunters, it seems to me to be rather and preferably an unfathomable (*abgrundliches*), rich sea—a sea full of motleyfish and crabs for which even the gods might long and become fishers and casters of nets: so rich is the world in strange things, great and small!

Not the violence and danger of hunting, but baiting hooks and casting nets constitute the parasitic economy. Are there really any beasts of prey, any strong, daring eagles who swoop down on innocent lambs? Yes, but isn't that "jungle" really part of the larger economy of the sea where big fish eat little fish in what from a macroscopic perspective is more regular and inclusive of the "jungle"?

Zarathustra squanders his animal metaphors as he details his search for "human fishes" with "glistening bait." Yet everything in this text "for his friends" will revolve around variations on feeding and playing the host. Far from beginning by *excluding* the parasites, as the preliminary notes suggest, the story communicated to the "friends" is one in which food is used to attract hangers-on of many sorts. The "friends of Nietzsche," whether Overbeck and his other select few or his readers since, including ourselves, also are being lured with such rich tasty food or bait. This, we may take it is part of Nietzsche's "greatest gift." When Nietzsche played with the title "Zarathustra's Temptation" (*Versuchung*) for Part Four we should recognize that that it can be read either as his temptation/seduction by pity or as the temptation/seduction exercised on the higher men, the friends, and the readers. And when Nietzsche tells everyone to keep quiet about the copies of *Zarathustra* IV that he is disseminating throughout the European postal system is he not also playing the "fisher of men," trying to instill each of the recipients (those who will bite) that he or she has a special relation to him like that of the higher men to Zarathustra? If that were so, then Nietzsche might be just as wary of the notion of friendship as is the latter. When Zarathustra says "O my friend, man is something that must be overcome" he suggests that only *Übermenschen*, not humans, can be true friends. And when he says that "woman is not capable of friendship" he explains that "women are still cats and birds. Or at best cows," quickly adding the question whether men are any better (Z, 83-84; 4, 72-73). Rather than friendship we have animal behavior, that is, parasitism, or as Nietzsche also calls it "love of the neighbor." The value of friendship oscillates; when Nietzsche, citing Emerson, writes that "friendship is to be overcome" it is an all-too-human friendship that is in question (*10, 512*). In declaring that men and women are not yet capable of friendship, it is the true friend of "the overflowing heart...in whom the world stands complete" who is invoked (Z, 88; 4, 78). Quite systematically, when friendship is spoken of in *Zarathustra*, the questions of whether men are different from animals and whether they are *capable* of friendship are also voiced, as in the talk "On the Compassionate":

> "My friends, your friend has heard a satirical saying: 'Just look at Zarathustra! Does he not go among us as if among animals?'
>
> But it is better said like this: 'The enlightened man goes among men *as* among animals.
>
> The enlightened man calls man himself: the animal with red cheeks'" (Z, 112; 4, 113).

But what is it to go among man as among animals? The value of the animal is sometimes that of the predator and sometimes that of the parasite; in any case nothing is more frequent in Nietzsche's writing than scorn for those who would fail to acknowledge the animal in human beings. What it means for Zarathustra to go among men as among animals should become clear once he has baited his hook and begun to catch a few.

After the honey sacrifice the noise begins. For the day following the episode of the honey sacrifice Zarathustra is alone again. Why? Because "the animals were roaming through the outside world to find new nourishment—also new honey, for Zarathustra had spent and squandered (*verthan und verschwendet*) the old honey down to the last drop" (Z, 254; 4, 300). He's behaving like a parasite; the animals are being forced to work overtime parasiting the bees. As Zarathustra sits there his thought, which we always suppose to be deep, is interrupted by a bit of visual noise—a shadow. It's the shadow of the Soothsayer. It's not high noon yet; at noon the shadows will be negligible but now they can get in the way. (Remember, Diogenes the Cynic told Alexander the Great that the one thing he could do for him was to get out of his light by removing his shadow.) There's going to be lots of noise now and the last in the series of higher men that Zarathustra nets not only will appear under the sign of the shadow but actually is Zarathustra's Shadow. The Soothsayer turns up before noon, at the time when morning shadows are still around. He's welcomed in terms that recall Greek laws of hospitality: "Welcome to you...not in vain shall you once have been my table- and guest friend (*Tisch und Gastfreund*). Eat and drink with me today also and forgive a cheerful old man for sitting down at table with you!" (Z, 255; 4, 301). Interrupted by the shadow of the Soothsayer, Zarathustra begins to hear the *Notschrei*, the cry of distress, that leads him on a zigzag course through his mountains. It's not only a sound, a cry, but an irresistible noise, the kind you have to do something about; it's "a long, long cry, which the abysses threw to each other and handed on, for none wanted to keep it: so evil did it sound" (Z, 255; 4, 301). It's like a siren, or like an automobile burglar alarm that can't be turned off, but renders all thought and concentration impossible. It's like a person who keeps call-

ing on the telephone, begging and soliciting, someone who
won't shut up and won't stop. It's both noise and a call (*Ruf*); it's
a call for Zarathustra, not the still, quiet call of conscience, but a
conference call of distress. The scene becomes more obviously
operatic as "the cry resounds again, longer and more protracted
and more anxiously (*ängstlicher*) than previously, and also much
closer than before." The Soothsayer knows that the call is for
Zarathustra and that whoever it is won't stop ringing until he
answers: "Don't you hear it? You, Zarathustra, can't you hear
it?" called the Soothsayer, "this cry's for you, it's calling you:
come, come, come, it's high time!"

From this point on we might *hear* this story as an opera
that begins with an unwanted interruption, a call that keeps
coming back, an opera in which interruptions become indis-
cernible from plot. Nietzsche's recent editors, Colli and Montinari, think that *Zarathustra* IV was originally conceived as a collection of songs (14, 326, citing *11, 339*: "4. *Zarathustra*. These
are the Songs of Zarathustra, which he sung to himself so that
he could bear his final solitude"). Unlike the speakers in the
earlier parts of the text each of these interrupters makes his
own characteristic kind of noise. The Soothsayer sighs and
sighs, a quieter but insistent version of the *Notschrei* that he
presses Zarathustra to answer. The Zarathustra corporation is
in deep trouble as the noise signifies. When in distress, they
seem to say, let's all get together and talk about Zarathustra. All
these odd figures who have made or are making their careers
on the basis of Zarathustra's speeches are calling for help.
There's no answering machine to put off the higher man. As
soon as he sends one off to the cave another shows up with his
own complaint. *Mitleid*, pity is Zarathustra's final temptation;
that is, pity or compassion for his own parasites who have nest-
ed in his softest and tenderest parts.

It's worth noting that the cry of distress is repeated frequently with the visitors, or suitors for friendship, after the
Soothsayer's arrival. The cry is transitive in structure: as soon
as one of the higher men cries out and is found, the cry
resounds again and a new hunt is undertaken. Even when
there's no reference to the insufferable cry of distress itself, its
components are there. Wandering away from the Enchanter,

who he says at first "must surely be the higher man, that evil cry of distress came from him" (Z, 264; 4, 313), Zarathustra sees the last pope. He doesn't need to cry out because his very appearance speaks of his affliction. In any case his first words are a plea: "Whoever you may be, traveler, help one who has gone astray, a seeker, an old man who may easily come to harm here" (Z, 271; 4, 321–322). And if (at that moment) he doesn't utter the great cry of distress himself, he brings its equivalent into the scene, for he confesses to being frightened by "the howling of wild animals." There perhaps is something of the *fort!/da!* experience here. First a long cry, which might be represented O-O-O-O, a wail of longing and separation. Then, someone is found, a cause is discovered for the disturbance; *there* he is, there's a scene of recognition as the higher men present their various credentials and a momentary silence before it all begins again. Zarathustra plays the mother here, running after the crying infants, taking responsibility for the household; and then reassuring the criers with a promise of food, rest and play. This is the structure of Zarathustra's temptation—in both senses. What sounds at first like a purely accidental interruption acquires a sinister identity through repetition. From an economic point of view it appears to be a fundamental regression, in which the higher men succeed in taking charge of Zarathustra as imperious infants may lord it over their mother. That's not the whole story, of course, for eventually the higher men themselves will be made to vanish permanently (another child-like fantasy perhaps) when the lion roars, signaling their departure with a collective cry, "as if from a single throat." Let's recall also that this is part of Nietzsche's gift, a game of *fort!/da!* that he is having with his readers, asserting his own mastery by imposing this repetition on us.

And who are these parasites taken individually? Readers have found it difficult to resist the interpreter's temptation to identify them with figures like Wagner (*der Zauberer*) or Tolstoy (*der freiwillige Bettler*); the circumstances of "private publication," secrecy, and restricted distribution could suggest that Nietzsche was aiming at a final, retrospective settling of accounts with some of the people most important to him. In *The Case of Wagner*, for example, Nietzsche describes Wagner as

Alcyone

essentially an actor rather than a musician or dramatist, and in
Zarathustra IV the Enchanter (*Zauberer*) presents himself as a
poet and singer but is identified as a bad actor. At the same
time Nietzsche makes it clear that the analysis of Wagner is
emblematic:

> When in this essay I assert the proposition that Wagner is
> harmful, I wish no less to assert for whom he is neverthe-
> less indispensable—for the philosopher.... Through Wagn-
> er modernity speaks most intimately concealing neither its
> good nor its evil—having forgotten all sense of shame (*The
> Case of Wagner*, Preface; 6, 12).

So the hermeneutics that would see a settling of private
accounts here by means of a coded letter addressed to an exclu-
sive circle must be juxtaposed against Nietzsche's tendency to
make the analysis of the individuals in question paradigmatic
for an epoch. That Wagner (at some point) was Nietzsche's
friend raises the question of what such an allegedly private
communication "to his friends" about this former friend might
mean. Just as we might say that the Enchanter is both Wagner
and the artist of modernity, so we might suspect that in dis-
playing him in this way to his "friends" Nietzsche is saying
something like "Oh my friends, there are no friends" (a saying
Diogenes Laertius attributes to Aristotle).[22] Indeed, Zarathustra
had said almost this when lecturing earlier "On the Friend": "O
my friend, man is something that must be overcome." To say to
one's friend (a human being) that humanity must be overcome,
in a discourse that questions what is conventionally and traditionally called *friendship:* is this not to say, "Oh my friends,
there are no friends"? And in fact Zarathustra ends this address
"There is comradeship (*Kameradschaft*): may there be friendship" (Z, 84; 4, 73).

One thing that *The Case of Wagner* makes clear is that for
Nietzsche Wagner is not the rich, overflowing talent for which
his naive admirers mistook him. Much of the description of
Wagner is couched in an economic and culinary language that
locates him with respect to the poles of frugal giving to excess
and squandering. For example,

As long as we are still childlike, and Wagnerians as well, we consider Wagner himself rich, even as a paragon of a squanderer (*für einen Ausbund von Verschwender*), even as the owner of huge estates (*Grossgrundbesitzer*)in the realm of sound. He is admired for what young Frenchmen admire in Victor Hugo, "the royal largesse." Later one comes to admire both of them for the opposite reasons: as masters and models of economy, as *shrewd* hosts (*kluge Gastgeber*). Nobody equals their talent for presenting a princely table at modest expense. (*The Case of Wagner*, 8; 6, 31)

Part of what is emblematic about Wagner, then, is that he provides so much less nourishment than he pretends to. And since Wagner is a figure of modernity, this is a way of saying that the modern is a poor, economizing condition that no longer understands feasting, celebration and abundance. Clearly the epithet *Wagnerian* in Nietzsche is close to the meaning of *parasite;* but the paradox is that the host offers only the simulacrum of the great feast, himself being a parasite who has gathered together scraps of melody and legend without creating a dynamic order of his own. But this is also to say that Wagner does not know how to be a friend; he *acts* at being the *Gastgeber* or the *Grossgrundbesitzer* rather than providing for guests and friends as befits a proper host. At the end of the section just cited Nietzsche adds that "Wagner does not give us enough to chew on" and confesses that as far as his leitmotifs are concerned "I lack all culinary understanding for that. If pressed, I might possibly concede it the status of an ideal toothpick, as an opportunity to get rid of *remainders* of food." We know how Nietzsche develops this culinary discourse in *Ecce Homo* where he claims to have discovered his own proper food only in recent years. What may not be so evident is that all of this talk of food, guests and hosts is more than an idiosyncrasy; it is one of Nietzsche's ways of articulating the most general economic structures, including that economy within which the eternal recurrence can be sung and affirmed.

Consider now the activities of some of the higher men in so far as they can be placed within such an economy. The prophet or Soothsayer (*der Wahrsager*) who warns Zarathustra

that the waters of distress are rising to his mountain is the first
to demand supper, insisting that hunger is his specific form of
distress. The two kings are the only guests rich or thoughtful
enough to bring something for the banquet, having loaded
their ass with wine. Still, they are not strong enough in their
traditional role as *Gastgeber* to provide a full banquet themselves. The very fact that there are *two* of them suggests that the
royal authority and beneficence have been diluted. They multiply like parasites. The Shadow, the unemployed last pope, and
the Ugliest Man are all parasites: the Shadow is a weak emana-
tion of Zarathustra, the pope is at loose ends now that his former boss and host is dead; the Ugliest Man is a mendicant
resentfully dependent on the pity of others. These guests provide only a bit of labor in helping to prepare the feast. The Voluntary Beggar requires an audience and is distressed that
everyone (at least in the human realm) refuses to accept him as
a preacher. On the whole these parasites have been displaced
from their attachment to God and have been seeking some substitute for that dependency, whether in nostalgia for aristocratic
values (the two kings), in the study of the parasitic brain itself,
or in the production of a new form of poetry that would
renounce any claims to truth (*der Zauberer*, posing as a *Büsser
des Geistes*). Zarathustra seems a likely substitute for what
they've lost. The appeal of banquet, warm cave, and companionship is palpable.

In his first greeting to the higher men who have collected
themselves at the cave, however, Zarathustra speaks and
behaves in a way to avoid simply taking the stable and benevo-
lent position that has been vacated by the old host. His greeting
to the assembled guests, whose voices can be heard as either
one or many cries of distress, proceeds on several different levels. On one, Zarathustra attempts to undermine the parasitic
relation of guests to host by a subtle diplomatic maneuver.
One's guests ought not to *feel* that they are parasites. He will
prove that these parasites who've invaded his solitude and
now noisily and uselessly occupy his home in fact have done
him a service, somewhat in the manner he had recommended
earlier in discussing the bite of the adder. What have they given
him? The feeling of strength that anyone can have in encourag-

ing one who despairs: "Even to me you gave this strength: a good gift (*Gabe*) my honored guests! A proper present to ensure hospitality! (*Ein rechtschaffenes Gastgeschenk!*) Well, then, do not be angry if I also offer you something of what is mine" (Z, 290; 4, 347). Even with parasites one observes the laws of hospitality: looking for some grounds of gratitude and begging the other not to be offended by one's presumption in offering something (always, in deprecation, "a little something") of one's own. Zarathustra offers them everything—his cave, the services of his animals, his guarantee of security—for the night. Do the guests hear this echo of the ambivalent way wishes are granted in the fairytale in his "you'll have everything, but for one night"? Everything is double edged or double coded here. To the friends, to the imaginary audience of the opera, the *Gabe* for which Zarathustra thanks his guests is also a dose, perhaps a dose of pity.

So on another level Zarathustra refuses the position of host. This is a melancholy, distressed crowd. What they need is a good shaking up. Zarathustra will not occupy the stable and centered position; he'll be the joker or wild card:

> Yet it seems to me you are poor company; you who utter cries of distress upset each other's hearts as you sit here together. First someone must come—someone to make you laugh again, a good merry clown (*Hanswurst*), a dancer and wind and wild cat, some old sort of fool (*Narr*)—what do you think? (Z, 290; 4, 347)

This is not the only time in *Zarathustra* IV that the host refers to himself as a *Hanswurst:* a clown, a buffoon, a figure of the carnival, a bloated sausage (called *Jack Pudding* in England and R. J. Hollingdale's translation; we might also think of Falstaff here).[23] The *Hanswurst* is an ambivalent figure within the logic of parasitism. He is a bloated parasite, fat from constant eating at others' tables and feasts; he never works. But he also is a target for the parasitism of others, a tempting meal for the hungry. At the carnival the excessive farewell to meat (*carne vale*) on the eve of Lent, the *Hanswurst* is emblematic of desperate, excessive, unlimited feasting; he is both the consumer and the consumed. The *Hanswurst* is a constant source of noise and disruption; at any moment he is likely to usurp the place of another and disorient things by his excess. As the permanent possibility of interruption and confusion, he has no identity that can itself be displaced as he displaces others. From the perspective of performance he is the anti-Wagnerian figure: promising very little and having no pretentions to be a *Grossgrundbeitzer*, he offers much more than the modern artist.

To struggle against pity and parasitism, Zarathustra must become the unpredictable noise that interrupts the interrupters. This pattern of interrupted interruptions is crucial to Part IV and especially to the ever-noisier festivities of the "last supper" and its aftermath. But the structure is announced, for example, in Zarathustra's first confrontation with *der Zauberer*. Although Zarathustra's attention was drawn to the cry of distress by the prophet, and he then accidentally ran into the two kings and the student of the leech's brain, the *Zauberer* is blatantly noisy and Zarathustra declares on seeing him that he "must indeed be the higher man: from him came that terrible cry of distress." Crying all the time, he pretends not to be interested in attracting an audience and feigns ignorance of Zarathustra's presence when he succeeds in getting it. His noise, or song, ostensibly is about his desertion by the unknown god. Now Zarathustra sees that this noise is really an attempt to capture *his* attention; the *Zauberer* is not merely a parasite lamenting the disappearance of his host, he is attempting at the moment to attach himself to Zarathustra. How does one handle such a parasite? Roughly.

> At this point, however, Zarathustra could not restrain himself any longer, raised his stick, and started to beat the moaning man (*den Jammernden*) with all his might. "Stop it," he shouted at him furiously. "Stop it, you actor! You counterfeiter!" (Z, 267-268; 4, 317)

(Could this stick be the magnificent staff which his disciples had given him earlier?)

Now the interruptions of the interruptions follow quickly on one another. *Actor* and *counterfeiter* are insults only on the supposition that one could act directly or produce genuine items of value. Otherwise one is a parasite. And like the other parasites this one justifies himself by quoting Zarathustra's own words. With the higher men Zarathustra hears his own words recited without comprehension. The parasites are also parrots and unconscious parodists. Yes, I *was* acting, the Enchanter confesses, but I acted the part that you devised yourself, that of the *Büsser des Geistes*, "the poet and Enchanter who at last turns his spirit against himself, the changed man who freezes to death from his evil science and conscience." Zarathustra had envisioned such modernist poets in the context of a parodic reference to Goethe in the speech "Of Poets"; he had told his disciple that the poets claim to be truthful when all they have to go on are their own metaphorical fantasies and that they create a false, parasitical union between themselves and their audiences. A reformed poet (what has been called a *modernist*) would be an ascetic or penitent who would be able to play on the liar's paradox and say, as Zarathustra does, "yes, the poets lie too much." These poets would confess their cognitive incapacity and their distance from their audiences. So Zarathustra provides a program for a modernist, hermetic, self-referential poetry. But one can noisily *play* at such a role, like the *Zauberer*, and from this we learn that no program or manifesto is sufficient for achieving artistic purity, should there be such a thing. Detected in his imposture this modernist *manqué* shifts the locus of the purity he seeks to Zarathustra, in the manner of all parasitic flatterers:

> "Did I test you? (*Versuchte ich dich?*) I—merely seek.
> O Zarathustra, I seek a genuine man, a proper simple, unequivocal man of all honesty, a repository of wisdom, a saint of knowledge, a great man!
> For do you not know, O Zarathustra? *I seek Zarathustra.*"
> (Z, 270; 4, 319)

This is an interesting series of epithets, and Zarathustra simply rejects the idea that there are such great men for others to parasite. But the Enchanter's distress, if not his flattery, is enough to earn him a dinner invitation.

The Enchanter with his tricks can hardly help reminding Nietzsche's "friends" of Wagner and thereby introducing an operatic dimension. But as Jacques Derrida says in another context, "all of Nietzsche's inquiries are coiled within the labyrinth of an ear," and this is certainly true of these meetings with the higher men, each of which has its own tone in both the literal and metaphorical senses.[24] The Soothsayer sighs and moans, like a whining echo of the cry of distress. When Zarathustra sees the two kings coming, he conceals himself and then interrupts them by speaking in a kind of stage whisper from his hiding place. Their speech resembles a comic interchange of Tweedledum and Tweedledee, for sometimes they are distinct voices and yet they can be provoked to speak in unison. Above all, they say they want to *hear* Zarathustra. Their ass begins its I-A braying in a parody of affirmation, and Zarathustra responds with a sudden, spontaneous, and sophomoric jingle about Christianity. The Conscientious Man makes himself known through cries and curses when Zarathustra trips over him as he hurries to answer the call; and like the other higher men he re-cites Zarathustra's own sayings to him. If we imagine this in recitative we must hear those sayings modulated through the misprisions of the assorted voices. The last pope, in begging for protection, speaks of his fears of the forest, intensified by the "howling of wild animals." From this point on Nietzsche's music drama can be punctuated by a cacophony of animal sounds, many of them specifically named, that form a counterpoint to the human cry of distress. These cries, howls, moans, and whispers would make this more than a merely human opera and force on its listeners the question of where the human belongs within a more general economy. It is the Ugliest Man who has the strangest voice of all the humans. Zarathustra can't bear to look at this wretch who killed God because *he* couldn't bear to be looked at. But remedies against his sounds are not so easily available as averting one's eyes from his terrible face. Not only his long speech in the sinister Valley of Snakes' Death but his crucial performance in the Ass Festival must be *heard* as a voice that is almost as "inexpressible" as his countenance:

> But then the dead wilderness resounded: for from the ground issued a gurgling, rattling (*röchelnd*) sound, such as water makes when it gurgles and rattles through

stopped-up water pipes at night: and at last a human voice and human speech emerged from it. (Z, 276; 4, 328)

This would be a wonderful challenge for the musical stage. We might be reminded of Arnold Schoenberg's post-Wagnerian, post-Nietzschean *Moses and Aaron* in which the extremities of the disarticulation of the voice are explored: Moses stutters (perhaps the only stuttering hero in opera) and the voice of God is split into a plurality of interweaving songs (so as not to violate the biblical prohibition of representing him). Like the stutterer, the Ugliest Man is a fountain of guttural consonants, consonants that as Serres suggests are the parasites of the voice:

> Articulated language begins with the sowing of consonants. But consonants are interruptions of the voice. Rupture, stopping, bifurcation of this flow. Yes, consonants are parasitic. They block the breath, cut it off, forbid it, close it, propel it, help it, modulate it.... Articulation is a set of strangulations; consonants strangle voices. They squeeze them.[25]

The long and difficult process by which the Ugliest Man starts up the strange hydraulics of his speech is repeated. After their first interchange we find these stage directions: "Thus spoke Zarathustra and made to depart; but the unutterable creature grasped for a corner of his garment and began again to gurgle and grope for speech (*nach Worten zu suchen*). 'Stay!' he said at last." From this voice, too, Zarathustra must hear his own words. What could be more maddening than to hear one's own speech repeated in tones, inflections, and accents that belie one's thoughts and feelings? Zarathustra, a speaker above all (as the lines above emphasize), encounters parasites who nest in his tenderest places: his speech, song, and articulation. After sending the Ugliest Man off to speak with his eagle and serpent, Zarathustra finds the Voluntary Beggar preaching to the cows; in performance this could be played for the contrast between a gentle, homiletic tone and the accompaniment of barnyard sounds. But such speeches drag things out, against Nietzsche's own dietary advice: "one should be warned against those long drawn out meals that I call interrupted sacrificial feasts—those of a *table d'hote*" (*EH*, 239; 6, 281). Refusing to eat their flesh and ministering to his herd, the preacher embodies the impossible attempt to opt out of the parasitic chain. He teaches that humans must become animal, and they must do so in order to transform their alimentary habits:

> "If we do not alter and become as cows, we shall not enter into the kingdom of heaven. For there is one thing we should learn from them: rumination (*Widerkauen*)... [man's] great affliction: that, however is today called *nausea* (*Ekel*). Who today has not his heart, mouth, and eyes filled with nausea? You too! You too! But regard these cows!" (*Z*, 280-281;4, 334).

The Voluntary Beggar is the theological counterpart of the Conscientious Man of the Spirit. Both the parasitologist and the principled vegetarian think that it is possible to remove themselves from the parasitic structure, either by adopting the stance of pure inquiry or by purifying one's diet. Each is, or becomes, Zarathustra's parasite. In enticing the Voluntary Beggar to the cave Zarathustra mentions the irresistible food: "You'll find new honey, too, at my cave, golden honey in the comb, cold as ice: eat it!" Honey is the parasite's perfect food, one that tempts even the ascetic and demonstrates that his way of becoming animal is not an exception to the general economy. The last guest acquired is the Shadow: an evanescent visual phenomenon, he interrupts Zarathustra by calling out to him to stop, echoing in a different key the visual interruption (the shadow) of the speaking guest (the Soothsayer or *Wahrsager*) who began this series.

At the dinner Zarathustra is host, buffoon, and *Hanswurst*. A talk by the host is in order, both because of the general nature of the occasion and because Zarathustra is a speaker. The talk "Of the Higher Man" follows a declensional or descending pattern that does not seem to meet the guests' expectations for a solemn lecture that would confirm their wisdom in seeking out their host. The speech is divided into three sequential parts. In the first Zarathustra reiterates the connection between the death of God and the demise of the doctrine of equality. If there is no God, there is no one before whom we are all equal; the order of rank based on the *Übermensch* replaces the divine hierarchy, so that higher men do indeed have their place. But in the second part of the talk Zarathustra gives practical, one might say mundane advice to the higher men, advice that may not be consistent with their exalted aspirations:

> "Follow in the footsteps of your fathers' virtue! How would you climb high the will of your fathers' did not climb with you?
>
> But he who wants to be a firstborn should see that he not also become a lastborn. And you should not pretend to be saints in those matters in which your fathers were vicious!
>
> He whose fathers passed their time with women, strong wine, and roast pork, what would it be if he demanded chastity of himself?" (Z, 302; 4, 363)

Sound advice, perhaps. But why *here*? To praise what Bakhtin calls the "lower stratum of the material body" is appropriate at a carnivalesque feast. Zarathustra is drawing attention to what's going on here and now; he's *not* meditating on the various forms of distress that have brought the higher men to where they are, but speaking of the parasitic activities of eating and drinking that actually engage them. From a structural point of view this speech "Of the Higher Men" occupies the same position in *Zarathustra* IV as Socrates' long speech on love in that other philosophical banquet and drinking party. Socrates' speech is marked by a double upward movement. First, in respect to the origin and authenticity of what is said, Socrates moves beyond the speeches of the other drinkers and diners to his own more philosophical account of love, and then finally to the divine mysteries of Diotima. Second, the content of those mysteries has to do with an ascending pattern of desire that rises from the realm of the sensory to beauty itself; the kinds of attractions found at a dinner party are at best the provocations of higher desires. But Zarathustra relentlessly moves down to the body, the body in its immediate context, in this speech that lacks any authority other than his own. The third and last part is a seduction and a provocation to laughter and dancing; to shaking up the body and heightening its openness to the rhythms of the party. If you've come to enjoy yourself at my expense, then let yourselves go, he says: "Lift up your hearts, my brothers, high, higher! And do not forget your legs! Lift up your legs too, you fine dancers; and better still stand on your heads!" (Z, 304-305; 4, 366).[26] "Stand on your heads"; so Nietzsche repeats in his own way the great philosophical imperative of the nineteenth century that has become a cliche in our accounts of Hegel and Marx. Heidegger, you recall, worries at some length whether Nietzschean inversion, turning things around, so that they stand on their heads, simply is a transformation within the limited and determinate set of possibilities that constitute Western metaphysics.[27] Did Nietzsche not perhaps, Heidegger asks, just begin to "twist free" rather than perform a technically agile but unconsciously scholastic and ultimately unadventurous headstand—when madness overtook him? Or should we think about the dancing to which Zarathustra exhorts the higher men, a dancing that Heidegger does not mention (so far as I know) and that he never thematizes. Even failures like *you*, Zarathustra says, you failures of Western metaphysics and parasites, can learn to dance.

From here on, the party is mostly noise. So noisy that it's hard to say just what happened. As the narrative eventually sums it up, commenting on the events around midnight:

> And what would you think then took place?...the old Soothsayer danced with pleasure; and even if, *as many of the chroniclers (Erzähler) think,* he was full of sweet wine, he was certainly fuller still of sweet life and had renounced all weariness. *There are even some who relate (erzählen)* that the ass danced at that time: for had the ugliest man given it wine to drink. This may be the case *or it may be otherwise;* and if in truth the ass did not dance that night, greater and stranger marvels than the dancing of an ass occurred. In brief, as the proverb of Zarathustra says: "What does it matter!" (Z, 327; 4, 396)

There was lots of noise at that party where Socrates spoke too; such a confusion that there are different versions, Plato's and Xenophon's. And Plato's is filtered through a series of narrators or chroniclers to compound the differences and the possibility of multiple stories.

It's after Zarathustra's speech "Of the Higher Men" that the interruptions intensify. The host runs out on the parasites, leaving them to gobble up whatever's left; Zarathustra needs fresh air. So the guests can make all the noise they want. In this last part of the story, Zarathustra is constantly in flight from the nausea that threatens to overtake him. In lecturing the higher men he had cried out *"Ekel! Ekel! Ekel!"* (Z, 298; 4, 358). Now he realizes that the parasites in his own cave are a provocation to *Ekel*. Outside the smells are better: "Oh pure odors (*Gerüche*) around me." And Zarathustra suggests a contrast between his own animals and the animallike behavior in the cave: "Tell me my animals: all these Higher Men—do they perhaps not *smell* well?... Only now do I know and feel how I love you, my animals" (Z, 306–307; 4, 369). Meanwhile the *Zauberer* is up to his old tricks, envious of his host's riches and eager to step between him and the higher men. That's what parasites do. The *Zauberer* here repeats Zarathustra's expression of nausea for he claims, like him and the other higher men, to suffer from *"the great nausea"* (Z, 307; 4, 370). Remember that after Socrates's great speech in the *Symposium* Alcibiades enters with his entourage, including his own flute-girl to disrupt the conversation. He's jealous of Socrates who's beginning to get close to Agathon, and he sits down between them, interrupting more than just the talk. The *Zauberer* sounds a bit like Alcibiades describing the lover who spurned him as a Silenus figure masking a beautiful god: "I also know this monster (*Unhold*) whom I love against my will, this Zarathustra: he himself sometimes seems to me like a beautiful mask of a saint, like a new strange masquerade in which my evil spirit, the melancholy devil, enjoys himself. I love Zarathustra, it often seems to me, for the sake of my evil spirit." Is *Zarathustra* IV parasitic on the *Symposium*, then, or is Nietzsche "twisting free" in some way we have yet to understand?

In both stories there is a competition in speech ranging from the lyrical and poetic to the discursive. Everyone sings for his supper, and each does so by speaking or poetizing—about love in the *Symposium*, about desire in *Zarathustra* IV. The movement upward in Plato is paralleled by one downward in Nietzsche's satyr play: up to the forms; down to the animal. Away with the flute-girls; cacophony among the guests. Zarathustra has addressed the question, "What is the desire of the higher men?" and tailored his remarks to the occasion of the feast. Now the *Zauberer* and Zarathustra's Shadow will offer their own poems of desire; the first will thematize and affirm the desire of the poet; the second will confess the impotence of European desire when confronted with the temptations represented by Oriental women. The *Zauberer* follows Zarathustra's implicit claims to truthfulness with a seductive lament praising the poet's desire as sharp and strong, like a beast of prey's, but acknowledging that gap between poetry and truth, that was named in "Of Poets":

> "The wooer of *truth*?" "You," so they jeered
> No! Only a poet!
> An animal, cunning, preying, creeping,
> That has to lie.
> That knowingly, willfully has to lie:
> Motley-masked,
> Lusting for prey, A mask to itself,
> A prey to itself—
> *That*, the wooer of truth?
> No! Only a fool! Only a poet!
> (Z, 308–309; 4, 371–372)

This song might remind us of another text that, like *Zarathustra* IV, Nietzsche withheld from publication. In "On Truth and Lie in an Extramoral Sense," he defined man as the tropological animal, who transforms all of his experiences into "a mobile army of metaphors, metonymies and anthropomorphisms"; this mobile army with the name of truth in fact is the primary weapon of a "clever animal" who desperately needs to control his environment and his fellow beasts. By playing with these tropes *as* tropes the poet achieves a certain freedom in comparison with the dogmatic scientist, but a freedom constantly at risk. Notice what the *Zauberer* gives up and what he retains; while abandoning any claim to truth and acknowledging himself as *"Nur Narr! Nur Dichter!"* he deploys a barrage of metaphorical animal identifications to body forth the poet's desire. In this part of *Zarathustra,* already chockfull of animals of one variety or another, he compares the poet to *"Ein Tier, ein listiges, raubendes, schleichendes,"* an eagle that pounces on lambs, a panther, and other companions of "speckled beasts of prey." If the poet is not the suitor of truth, we paraphrase, he at least is a noble, daring animal and not a cringing parasite:

> Thus
> Eagle-like, panther-like
> Are the poet's desires,
> Are *your* desires under a thousand
> masks,
> You fool! You poet!
> You saw man as god and sheep:
> To rend the god in man
> As the sheep in man,
> and in rending to laugh— (Z, 310; 4, 373)

Yet at the end of his song the *Zauberer* introduces a second type of image which gives the lie to his vision of himself as a *Raubtier,* when he compares himself to the moon:

> When the air grows clear,
> When the moon's sickle
> creeps along, green,
> Envious in the purple twilight,
> Enemy to day... (Z, 310; 4, 373)

Throughout *Zarathustra,* for example in "On Immaculate Perception," the moon is described as enviously parasitic on the light of the sun. Like the moon, the *Zauberer* has only a reflected truth to cling to, namely, he is banished from all truth. His desire is a parasitic desire. And he temporarily displaces Zarathustra, because "all who were present went like birds unaware into the net of his cunning and melancholy voluptuousness. Only the conscientious man of the spirit was not captured" (Z, 311; 4, 375). He charges that the magician is not a bird of prey but a cunning, stealthy trapper of birds. Not long before Zarathustra had compared the higher men to endangered birds when he warned them to be on their guard against the learned (*Gelehrten*) who "have cold, dried up eyes, before which all birds lie stripped of their feathers" (Z, 300; 4, 361). The Conscientious Man's reaction again sounds the note of nausea; it's appropriate that it should be sniffed out by the parasitologist in the group: "Air! Let in good air! Let Zarathustra in! You are making this cave sultry and poisonous (*schwül und giftig*), you evil old sorcerer!" (Z, 311; 4, 375). Although he does not know it, this is the Conscientious Man's greatest contribution to the study of "the brain of the leech. "

The question posed by this forcible interruption—for the Conscientious Man has snatched the Enchanter's harp from him—is whether a scientific observation of the parasite can itself escape the logic of parasitism. The desire is to establish a resting place, a point of stability from which order will unfold. Just as the Conscientious Man wants the clean air and the distanced perspective of science, so the Enchanter would find a similar satisfaction of closure in his art. Savoring his artistic triumph he denounces the *noise* of the interruption, as the other had voiced his disgust with the *smell* of his song: "'Be quiet!' he said in a modest voice, 'good songs want to echo well (*gute Lieder wollen gut wiederhallen*); one should be long silent after good songs.'" But can songs echo well in a world of noisy parasites? In the host's absence, they begin to grab for each others' things, to contest each others' places, to compete to make the most noise. The parasitical function is completely transitive.

Zarathustra comes back, refusing the subterfuges of both the melancholy song and the scientist's praise of the security of knowledge as antidote to fear. Again he piles interruption on interruption. Neither science nor "The Melancholy Song" will be able to resound by itself, for the host manages to dissolve the spat between the guests "into a great peal of laughter." The Enchanter replies with an ambivalent encomium in which he praises Zarathustra for loving his enemies while taking revenge on his friends, thus insinuating that the higher men are indeed his friends. But are they? The text dances coyly around this question:

> Thus spoke the old Enchanter, and the Higher Men applauded him: so that Zarathustra went round and mischievously and lovingly (*mit Bosheit und Liebe*) shook hands with his friends—like one who has to make amends and apologize to everyone for something. As he came to the door of his cave, however, he already felt again a desire for the good air outside and for his animals, and he was about to slip out (Z, 313; 4, 378).

What kind of "friends" are these that awaken the stirrings of nausea once more?

The Shadow, perhaps the neediest and most parasitic of the parasites, successfully begs his host to stay; the great cry of distress has become a very specific plea. The Shadow has his own song to sing; he usurps the place of the last parasite as he seizes the harp that the *Zauberer* had just played and the Conscientious Man had snatched away; such comic circulation of emblems makes visible the metastable logic of parasitism and mimics the circulation of the gift. Ostensibly the wilderness or wasteland (*die Wüste*) that is the setting of the Shadow's song is an oriental desert graced by dancing girls; but the warning that frames the song suggests that the wasteland is an internal threat: "The wasteland grows: woe unto him that harbors wastelands!" As did the Enchanter, this singer implies that his song is an antidote to *Ekel*. In begging Zarathustra to stay he appeals to his pity: "Don't go! Otherwise the old, dull affliction (*die alte dumpfe Trübsal*) may again assail us" (Z, 314; 4, 379). The Shadow entreats Zarathustra with the promise of "good air...good, clear, oriental air" in fact the dry air of the desert. In this progression of songs there is an increasing emphasis on the *materiality* of voice, breath and articulation, a materiality that had, characteristically, been effaced in the Enchanter's attempt to impersonate a beast of prey. "With his nostrils, however, he drew in the air slowly and inquiringly, like someone tasting strange air in strange lands. Thereupon he began to sing with a kind of roaring (*Gebrüll*)" (Z, 315; 4,

380). The song doubles itself by naming this very roaring which its story will undercut:

> A worthy beginning!
> Solemnly in an African way!
> Worthy of a lion
> Or of a moral screech-ape...

Whereas the Enchanter had attempted to appropriate the healthy aura of beasts of prey, the Shadow borrows their sounds while confessing that his internal desert is not worthy of them. Like T. S. Eliot's *The Wasteland*, separated from this one by forty years and World War I, this poem is a cry of cultural and erotic devastation; it is a confession of the impotence of the parasite that relies on a complex series of references to Europe and Europe's view of its other. The plans for *Zarathustra* IV name the Shadow figure "the good European" and throughout the song he represents himself as the destined development of an exhausted European tradition attempting to nourish itself from the vital east (a gesture repeated in a more religious key by Eliot in his invocation of Hindu and Buddhist doctrines of salvation). This poem of desire begins by explicitly contrasting the singer with animals (the lion or even the "moral howling monkey") that might ennoble him through association. So the Shadow begins with a gesture of more profound renunciation than the *Zauberer* did. He claims no part of the world of fierce animal desire. He wants to be eaten, he yearns to be swallowed, by the oasis or by the girls. He fantasizes about being consumed. After all, what's left when one is immobilized by doubt, the nihilistic legacy of European philosophy spawned by the Cartesian gesture?

> ...however I doubt it,
> since I come from Europe,
> Which is more sceptical than
> any little old wife.

What "European dignity" can do is roar morally before the daughters of the wasteland. But this moral roaring is merely a cover for an impotence that has its own specifically Protestant, Lutheran roots:

> For virtuous howling,
> You dearest maidens,
> Is loved best of all by
> European ardor, European hunger!
> And there I stand even now
> As European,
> I can do no other; God help me!
> Amen!

Europe would be a parasite on the east; but it lacks the strength for even a parasitic assault. It is not the desire of the bird or beast of prey but the desire to be consumed that takes command.

In one of the notes of 1883 Nietzsche writes *"In Zarathustra 4 kein 'Ich'!"* (10, 545). In the downward movement of the *Narrenfest* Zarathustra has been displaced by his own shadow, who seems to fulfill the nihilistic prophecies of *der Wahrsager* in Zarathustra's first encounter with a "higher man." Zarathustra has asked, "Who will be the lords of the earth?" and the good European has replied that he can't find the strength even for these alluring and accessible dancing girls. It gets noisier; the parasites are having a field day now that they've come out into the open and confessed what they are. Zarathustra leaves again; who can stand the noise and the smell of such people, he asks the animals? But noise is a useful signal of the arrival or the flourishing of parasites. In 1883 Nietzsche was taking notes on a book by Alfred Espinas, on *Animal Societies*, which undertakes a systematic categorization of the forms of animal community. Espinas argues that there can be no community among animals of different species and begins his account with what he takes to be the most degenerate case of animal interaction, namely parasitism. Nietzsche's notebooks contain a number of entries that explicitly or implicitly develop some of these themes, for example:

> The parasite is the essential kernel of vulgar feeling.
> The feeling of receiving nothing without giving something in return is the noble feeling. Nothing else! No

"grace" (*Gnaden*)! But also no suffering, no — (*10*, 294; Nietzsche leaves the space indicated by the dash open).

Nietzsche here is parasiting both Espinas and Emerson on parasitism, as I am parasiting Michel Serres. Emerson had written in "Compensation": "He is great who confers the most benefits. He is base—and that is the one base thing in the universe—to receive favors and render none.... Beware of too much good staying in your hand. It will fast corrupt and worm worms. Pay it away quickly in some sort."[28] What is notable in Nietzsche's formulation is the *exclusion*: nobility is *nothing else but* the disposition to always give something when one receives. And social institutions are to be interpreted in terms of some forms of parasitism and symbiosis:

> The *removal* of *parasitic* men is the meaning of punishment. Birds that protect a buffalo from parasites live off of them,—and the buffalo is grateful that they announce the arrival of an enemy.—Meaning of the *police*. (Espinas p. 159; *10*, 318)

Noise may announce the arrival of the parasite and we must be grateful for the parasite of the parasite.

Where is Zarathustra in all of this noise, in this exchange of places and jostling for position? He's outside now, or perhaps we should say that in *Zarathustra* IV he's inside and outside; he's the joker and the *Hanswurst*. Is this what is meant by "*In Zarathustra 4 kein ' Ich'!*"? Is he like the cursor in the word processor, running through all of the possible positions and simply reminding the reader of where she is now in the midst of all the noise? Zarathustra becomes the interruption himself when he leaves and returns, which is his repeated action at his own party. He's the host so powerful that he can abandon his own *potlatch*; he doesn't need to be there to receive the admiration and envy of his guests. Still outside he takes their loud rejoicing (*Jubel-Lärm*), their shouting and their laughter as a sign of the success of the dinner. There's a connection, Zarathustra asserts, between proper food and healthy sounds:

"My man's fare (*Manns-Kost*), my succulent and strength-
ening discourse is effective: and truly, I did not feed them
with distending vegetables (*Bläh-Gemüsen*)! But with war-
riors' food, with conquerors' food: I awakened new
desires." (*Z*, 320; *4*, 387)

Bläh-Gemüse would have induced flatulence rather than shouts
and laughter. Here Zarathustra reminds us of the high and the
low ends of the food/noise connection.

When he comes back, this time, it's noisier than ever with
all of the higher men worshiping the ass. In the descent from
high to low, in the inversion of values, this is about as far as
they can go. The beast of burden brought by the kings becomes
the new mediator. Replacing Christ by the figure of the ass is a
standard feature of the medieval-Renaissance carnivalesque
tradition; Bakhtin describes it very well.[29] At the carnival all the
parasites come out to play and they turn everything upside
down, making a *verkehrte Welt*. We might think of the degrada-
tions at that prophetic feast of Belshazar, recounted in the *Book
of Daniel*. But here the worship of the idol is not followed by
divine punishment. The ass is the figure of all that we parasite;
it is a beast of burden, down at the bottom of the chain. Not as
respectable as the bees who have a miraculous product and an
organized society, the ass, as the litany makes clear, is beaten
and abused. As Serres remarks: "Everything begins with what I
call abuse value. The first economic relation is of abuse."[30]
What is worth thinking about here is that the positions of noise
and significant speech have been reversed and transformed.
Ordinarily the braying of the ass, I-A, hee-haw, and so on, is a
sheer interjection, sometimes comic, sometimes annoying. The
ass, as Nietzsche never tires of reminding us, has very big ears,
because he is receptive to sound in all of its noisy crudity rather
than to the subtle differentiations of tone and style for which
small ears are designed. When Zarathustra returns to his own
cave, where the stage has now been set for the ass festival, he
eventually becomes the interrupting noise in relationship to the
braying of this divinized ass. But before that he is shocked by
the sudden silence in the cave: "But suddenly Zarathustra's ear
was startled (*Plötzlich aber erschak das Ohr Zarathustra's*). In this

concatenation of noises, voice, and music, silence itself can have the disturbing effect that the cry of distress once had.

The I-A of the ass bears a relationship, if only a parodic one, to the affirming *Ja* of the thought of eternal recurrence, "the highest possible formula of affirmation." But whatever is voiced here is uttered as static: "Just then the ugliest man began to gurgle and snort (*zu gurgeln und zu schnauben*) as if something inexpressible wanted to get out of him; but when he really found words, behold, it was a pious, strange litany" (Z, 321; 4, 388). In this litany the ass is praised for braying, not speaking, and for having long ears. In his gurgling and snorting distortion of speech, that is in his parasitic noise, the ugliest man has become the hierophant who conducts the litany and we regularly hear that *"Der Esel aber schrie dazu I-A."* In this world of sounds it is the affirmation of the discordant, the grating and the incoherent that is being performed. Not only is the rite uttered in the disgusting voice of the Ugliest Man and the cry of the donkey, but the sounds of Nietzsche's texts set up a sliding or shifting between *Ekel* and *Esel*, between nausea and the "redeemer" from the great nausea. Which is the noise and which is the message here? If the ass does indeed "always say *Ja* to the world he created" has the thought of thoughts been transformed into noise? Or is it always already noise? Remember that in "The Convalescent" when the animals profess to tell Zarathustra what is his thought he dismisses them as barrel organs who have made a hurdy-gurdy song (*ein Leierlied*) out of his thought or, at best, a pretext for chattering (*Schwätzen*) or music. To their first approaches to him after he regains speech he replies: "For me—how should there be any outside-of-me? There is no outside! But all *sounds (Tönen)* make us forget this; how lovely it is that we forget. Have not *names and sounds* been given to things that man might find things refreshing? *Speaking* is a beautiful folly" (Z, 234; 4, 272). In *The Birth of Tragedy* Nietzsche had written that traditional opera was constituted by parasitism; that is, by making words and dialogue more important than music, it reversed the proper relationship (BT, 19; 1, 125–126). Eventually Wagner, too, is said to be a parasite, even though he seemed to restore music to its proper place of honor. But in *Zarathustra* IV it's no longer a question of identifying parasite and host once and for all by means of a fixed binary system of values. Now either words or music may be interuped by the other. Parasitism has been transvalued in a world of noise.

When the thought of eternal recurrence is voiced in *Zarathustra* it is either in the mouth of animals (the eagle and the serpent in chorus, the I-A of the ass) or it comes from a throat that is uncanny and barely human (we might compare Nietzsche's repeated description of the *gurgelnd* and *röchelnd* voice of the Ugliest Man with the uncanny speech of Poe's M. Valdemar who says *"I am dead"*) or with the sneering voice of the distorted creature of a vision (the dwarf). In the concluding scenes of the mock opera that is *Zarathustra* IV, the thought is sung, gurgled and brayed but never spoken; it is the preeminent thing that Zarathustra does *not* say in this book of speeches. At the one point in the book when we might suspect Zarathustra of uttering the thought, he whispers something in Life's ear:

> "you think, Oh Zarathustra, I know it, you think of leaving me soon!" "Yes," I answered hesitatingly, "but you also know...." And I said something into her ear, in the midst of her tangled, yellow, foolish tresses. "You *know* that, Oh Zarathustra? No one knows that." (Z, 243; 4, 285)

Is the thought too secret, too esoteric to be vulgarized and divulged? This fourth part of *Zarathustra*, as we've already seen, occupies an undecidable space in relation to the public and the private. Posted to a small circle of "friends," it is mentioned in the philosopher's published writings; but its claims to a hermetic character are undercut by its playing with the forms of the drama, the festival, and the opera—the most public of events. Within this story itself the thought is voiced in many ways, so that a strict secrecy is hardly maintained, although the question of what is being uttered is certainly complicated and intensified. *The thought is never spoken by a human voice;* even in its first published appearance in *The Gay Science* we are to suppose that a demon were to come to us with the thought in our "loneliest loneliness" (*GS*, 341).

Perhaps Nietzsche is suspicious of a certain set of metaphysical positions that cluster around the concept of the human voice. What could be more immediate, more present to us, so this tradition intones, than our own voice and breath? Perhaps our thought, if anything. The proper embodiment of a human thought is a human voice.[31] But what if the thought in question is one that puts in question these very values of presence and immediacy? To think through the thought of eternal recurrence is to realize that it requires a rethinking of the concepts of presence and absence. There is no pure presence, it suggests, no substantial self, no eternal forms or concepts, no absolute knowledge; there are only the moments in their becoming and their passage. The moment (*Augenblick*) is not present but it is deep, infinitely deep. To give voice to this thought as if one were now explaining what was really and truly present, as opposed to all of those false candidates for presence in the metaphysical and theological traditions, would be to betray the thought.

In *Zarathustra* there is a complex network of visual and auditory ways of "presenting" this thought of nonpresence. We should begin by noticing the contrast between the visual, schematic images and those addressed to the ears. In "Of the Vision and the Riddle" the dwarf provides a succinct account that could easily be translated into a banal pedagogy of the blackboard: "'Everything straight lies,' murmured the dwarf disdainfully. 'All truth is crooked, time itself is a circle'" (Z, 178; 4, 200). And in "The Convalescent," the animals employ similar images, although in celebratory tones: "Existence begins in every instant; the ball There rolls around every Here. The middle is everywhere. The path of eternity is crooked" (Z, 234; 4, 273). What does Zarathustra reject in rejecting these two versions of the circle, that favorite philosophical diagram to which the tradition from Plato and Aristotle to Hegel keeps circling back? He refuses to accept an account of the thought that would suppose the availability of a God's eye point of view, a perspective of all perspectives, from which the circle of existence could be mapped. What the diagram cannot represent is the infinite depth of each of the points that compose the circle, not to mention the complex form of continuities and discontinuities by which they are affiliated or separated.

And what of the thought of thoughts? It may be worth rereading the first sentences of the section on *Zarathustra* in

Ecce Homo, a section that, by the way, maintains its silence on the noise of *Zarathustra* IV, explicitly affirming that the third part was the inspired completion of the work. But Nietzsche begins by writing:

> Now I shall relate (*erzähle*) the history (*Geschichte*) of *Zarathustra.* The fundamental conception (*Grundconception*) of this work, the idea of the eternal recurrence, this highest formula of affirmation that is at all obtainable, belongs in August 1881: it was penned on a sheet with the notation underneath "6000 feet beyond man and time." That day I was walking through the woods along the lake of Silva-plana; at a powerful pyramidal rock not far from Surlei I stopped. It was then that this idea came to me.
>
> If I reckon back a few months from this day, I find as an omen a sudden and profoundly decisive change in my taste, especially in music. Perhaps the whole of *Zarathustra* may be reckoned as music; certainly a rebirth of the art of *hearing* was among its preconditions (*EH*, 295; 6, 335).

And just a page or so later Nietzsche is at pains to make sure that proper credits are passed out for the composition of the *Hymn to Life* (for mixed chorus and orchestra), text by Lou Salomé, music by Nietzsche. He adds, "Perhaps my music, too, attains greatness at this point. (Last note of the A-clarinet, c-flat, not c: misprint)." So the *Grundconception* of *Zarathustra*, the eternal recurrence, is buried among noise, music, and attributions: the noise of the press that regularly produces misprints, the noise of the reception process that could mistake Lou's text for Nietzsche's. Even the site of the inspiration has been mistaken (as Walter Kaufmann's footnote points out) by people who have misidentified the fateful rock.[32] And what, after all, is a *Grundconception*? Note that Nietzsche does not describe the thought in question as a *Begriff* or as an *Idee* but rather as the key to a book. *Concept*, in German usage, refers not to philosophical ideas or concepts, but to sketches, outlines, germs of stories and so on. A *Konzeptbuch* is a sketchbook. Perhaps it's a bit like the use in English of *concept* to designate the nerve of a new popular movie or of an advertising campaign.

Which is the voice, the noise, the music? The thought of eternal recurrence, the buffoonery of the story, the parodic recapitulation of and perhaps the twisting free from Platonic philosophy—all these seem to occupy these positions in turn. After listening to the litany, we read or hear: "Zarathustra could no longer master himself; he cried out I-A louder even than the ass, and sprang into the midst of his guests gone mad" (Z, 322; 4, 391). Zarathustra's I-A is or could be the genuine affirmation as opposed to the degenerate omnisatisfaction of the ass; the signal that he, by imitating the ass's bray, is ready to enter into a new song competition; and the interruption, the noise that breaks off the festival, that had itself been part of the noise of the party. Under this last description his intervention is the interruption of an interruption, the noise that disrupts the noise of his parasitic guests. Zarathustra gives his blessing to the *Eselfest*, finally, and says that this and "some old gay fool of a Zarathustra" is just what the higher men need—and laughter.

The noise rises to a crescendo in "The Drunken Song," which begins with the Ugliest Man, transfigured, affirming eternal recurrence with his gurgles and snorts. More precisely, we might say that the Ugliest Man poses the *question* of eternal recurrence and its affirmation. This way of posing the question is notable both for its voicing—its gurgling and snorting—as well as for its form of address, for he calls the higher men surrounding him (and Zarathustra, too, we suppose) his friends:

"My assembled friends," said the Ugliest Man, "what do you think? For the sake of this day—*I* am content for the first time to have lived my whole life.

"And it is not enough that I testify only this much. It is worth while to live on earth: one day, one festival with Zarathustra has taught me to love the earth.

"'Was that life?'" I will say to death. 'Very well! Once more!'

"My friends, what do you think? Will you not, like me, say to death: 'Was that—life? For Zarathustra's sake, very well! Once more!'" (Z, 326; 4, 395–396).

The Ugliest Man speaks the thought of eternal recurrence. In his notes Nietzsche writes: "In *Zarathustra* 4: the great thought as *the head of Medusa:* all the features of the world become rigid, a frozen struggle with death (*Todeskampf*)" (11, 360). Like the head of Medusa, the Ugliest Man generally is an unbearable sight, although he now is transfigured. The thought, taken as an image or a picture, could paralyze the seer or the thinker, for it inscribes nausea in the very countenance of life. Frozen into the last moments of a death agony the only way to understand the eternal recurrence would be the impossible utterance "I am dead." But the inexpressibly disgusting can be transformed by the pluralizing, differentiating proliferation of voices, sounds, music and noise.

When Nietzsche first broached the thought of eternal recurrence it was by means of a story in which each of us was to imagine how we would respond should a demon come to us in our loneliest loneliness. Now, in what is arguably the most explicit affirmation of the thought by a human voice, albeit in the form of a strangled expectoration, it is still a question but one addressed to "friends." But do not other questions arise here? Can there be a friendship of or around the thought of eternal recurrence? Is some radical misunderstanding implicit in the idea that this thought could provide a bond, a tie of *philia*, centered around the person of Zarathustra? For if the ultimate consequence of thinking this thought is to make the thinker an *other* (as the demon says) then *who* precisely will enter into this friendship? Or how can a friendship "prior" to the grappling with this thought be expected to survive when the thinkers have become other? This thought always brings a lot of static along with it. And just at this point, the point where the parasites are on the verge of transfiguration, the narrative becomes self-questioning and deconstructs itself (in the vulgar sense) by expressing its own inability to decide among the many visions of what happened next. Even Zarathustra's thoughts, or perhaps we should say *especially* Zarathustra's thoughts, are inaccessible at this point. After this incident we hear (in a narrative that has just confessed its own inability to decide among competing versions of a confused and confusing series of events): "Zarathustra...stood there like one intoxicated: his eyes grew dim, his tongue stammered, his feet tottered. And who could divine what thoughts then passed over Zarathustra's soul?" (Z, 327; 4, 396–397).

Could these thoughts be questions about the possibility of the friendship invoked by the Ugliest Man as well as his parasitic noises and his parasitic repetition of a text on repetition? In this world of noise and generalized parasitism, everything shimmers and becomes undecidable. Does this undecidability extend to the remaining ten pages or so of the text, marked as they are by new sounds, music, and noises? We can imagine Zarathustra hearing an echo at this point of Beethoven and Schiller's "*O Freunde, nicht diese Töne!*" The new tones include the sound of the bell that comes up *slowly* at midnight, a midnight song that is whispered, that "laughs in a dream," a speech that can be only for "delicate ears." It's whispered so softly, played on such a "sweet lyre" with the sound of a "drunken ranunculus croaking (*trunkenen Unken-Ton*)" that we always may be unsure just what we heard, even if we listen to Mahler's exquisitely soft rendition of the "*Das Nachtwandler-Lied*" And after whispering and teaching the lines of this song one by one Zarathustra says or whispers:

> Have you now learned my song? Have you guessed its intent? Well then, you higher men, sing me now my round.
> Now sing yourselves the song whose name is "Once More" (*Noch ein Mal*) whose meaning is "To all eternity!"—sing, you higher men, Zarathustra's roundelay! (Z, 333; 4, 403)

So the eternal recurrence is a song, a ditty. It is mixed with music and noise here, just as Nietzsche recalls it later in *Ecce Homo*, sandwiched between his new sense for music and his notes on the Salomé-Nietzsche "Hymn to Life." In the twelve sections by which the individual lines of "*Das Nachtwandler-Lied*" are presented before being sung *da capo*, there are an extraordinary number of indications of tonal variation and mood to articulate the differences that this song of "deep eternity" orchestrates and implies, for at midnight "many a thing can be heard which may not speak by day" (Z, 328; *4*, 398). The emphasis could be put on the *many:* to think (hear) the eternal recurrence is to think (hear) both the static and the melody of the moment. Among these musical directions we read

> it sighs! how in dreams it laughs!…do you not hear how secretly, fearfully, warmly it speaks to you…. The day howls…the wind falls silent…the graves mutter: "Redeem the dead! Why is night so long? Does the moon not intoxicate us?"…the bell booms, the heart still drones…. Sweet lyre! I love your tone your drunken ranunculus-tone—from how long ago, from how far away does your sound come to me…a midnight lyre, a croaking bell (*Glocken-Unke*) that no one understands, but which *has* to speak before the deaf…is the wind not a dog? It whines, it yelps, it howls. Ah! Ah! how it sighs! how it laughs and gasps, the midnight hour! How it now speaks soberly, this drunken poet…. "What has become perfect, everything ripe—wants to die!" thus you speak (Z, 328-31; *4*, 398-401).

As Zarathustra says or sings during the song itself "this discourse (*Rede*) is for delicate ears," and he says this at the point where the song asks *"what does deep midnight's voice say? (was spricht die tiefe Mitternacht?)"* (Z, 329; *4*, 399). So it's a question of who sings and how one listens. Don't sing like a raucous parasite, Zarathustra says, sing softly and subtly like me. And you must sing it in your own voices, with gurgles and snorts, with the histrionics of the *Zauberer,* and the apologetic ironies of the Shadow. But this voicing *may or may not occur,* for all we can tell from the text that simply assembles this *Rundgesang* as a whole. Do the higher men lend their voices to the midnight hour or does Zarathustra sing the song again, *da capo,* in a whisper or with power and timbre? We don't know. Everyone was drunk. Each remembers it differently. In any case the parasites, bloated, sated, and exhausted as they are, sleep late the next morning. In the chapter called "The Sign" that ends this last part of the book, Zarathustra makes it clear that what constitutes a sign for discerning ears does not necessarily signify for another. The signs in question are essentially auditory:

"I want to go to my work, to my day: but they do not understand what are the signs (*Zeichen*) of my morning, my step—is no wake-up call (*Weckruf*) for them.

"They are still sleeping in my cave, their dream still drinks at my midnight songs (*Mitternachten*). The ear, that listens (*horcht*) to me, the *obeying* ear (*das gehorchende Ohr*) is lacking in them (Z, 333; 4, 405).

Although he had heard the cry of need all too vulnerably, they sleep through the morning alarm clock. The punning that Zarathustra indulges in, unheard by their sleeping ears, recalls his declaration during the song itself that the parasites will not *hear* him aright. The sign or signs that Zarathustra detects now manifest themselves primarily and in the first instance as auditory; this can easily be overlooked, because of the visual bias of our thought about interpretation that easily can lead us to produce imagined pictures of the swarm of birds and the laughing lion that Zarathustra encounters. But after noting the deafness of the higher men, Zarathustra "heard above him the sharp cry of his eagle" and then "he suddenly heard that he was surrounded by countless birds, swarming and fluttering—the whirring of so many wings and the throng about his head, however, were so great that he shut his eyes" (Z, 334; 4, 406). Here, if anywhere, in a concluding chapter with the possibly portentous title of "The Sign" we ought to listen and read carefully—*buchstäblich*. The sound of the sign forces Zarathustra to shut his eyes. The eyes of the higher men are shut at this point, too, but shut because they're oblivious to sound whereas Zarathustra is receptive to it. It's as if a "cloud of love" has taken away Zarathustra's sight, like the clouds under which the Greek gods sometimes conducted their amours; "and behold, in this case it was a cloud of love, and over a new friend." Zarathustra's eyes are still closed, he's disoriented while warding off the birds; it's now that he announces the coming of the sign:

behold, then something even stranger occurred: for…he clutched unawares a thick, warm mane of hair; at the same time, however, a roar rang out in front of him—the gentle, protracted roar of a lion. *"The sign comes,"* said Zarathustra, and his heart was transformed. (Z, 334; 4, 406)

He offers his own interpretation of the sign: *"My children are near, my children."* But no children appear in the text, although there is talk of "a new friend," the laughing lion, and of Zarathustra's heart being loosened. There's something unspeakable about these forms of friendship and affection now suggested by the sign. This is the time for the disappearance of the illusory friends, the higher men, who came to seduce him to his last sin, pity. And they finally wake up, perhaps (although we're not told) because of all the noise outside the cave. Their disappearance takes place through a complex series of noises, signals, and countersignals:

> But when they reached the door of the cave and the sound (*Geräusch*) of their steps preceded them, the lion started violently, suddenly turning away from Zarathustra, and leaped up to the cave, roaring fiercely (*wild brüllend*); the Higher Men, however, when they heard its roaring, all cried out as with a single mouth and fled back and in an instant had vanished (*im Nu verschwunden*). (Z, 335; 4, 407)

This is the old cry of distress, the last in a series of repetitions brought to an end by the coming of friends and children. The parasites have been reduced to a single noisy function. Zarathustra's question asks not what he saw but, "What was it I heard? What has just happened to me?" The suggestion of the term *das Zeichen* is that of a portent or announcement that can be understood by one in possession of the proper code. Yet at each stage in this episode of *"Das Zeichen,"* Zarathustra is disoriented or surprised by a sound. The night before he had orchestrated a song at midnight for the higher men, while telling them that they could not understand it, that they lacked the *ears* for it. Now he's listening to sounds himself, hearing meanings in them as the Greeks heard oracles in the rustling of leaves. Zarathustra has perfected his ears. The function of the lion's roar has been to close the circle of parasitism. It is Zarathustra's beast, his own noisemaker with which he'll disrupt the scrambling, chattering higher men. (The Shadow played with a lion's roar that he could not sustain.) Remember La Fontaine's story of the city rat and the country rat. When the tax collector comes home and makes a noise the parasites scatter. Serres hears this as the only kind of closure attainable in a world of parasitism:

> The parasited one parasites the parasites. One of the first, he jumps to the last position. But the one in the last position wins the game.
> He has discovered the position of the philosopher.[33]

This is hardly an absolute closure; it is a temporary consideration in a metastable pandemonium. Pan*demon*ium: not just one demon comes to whisper to us in our loneliest loneliness, but that whisper (like Zarathustra's in Life's ear), proliferates into sounds of every sort. The lion's roar is the last sound—for now. But there are those birds, fluttering and swarming; what will happen when we listen to their cries?

Notes

1. Eugen Fink, *Nietzsches Philosophie* (Stuttgart, 1960), pp. 114, 118.

2. Lawrence Lampert, *Nietzsche's Teaching* (New Haven, 1986), p. 287.

3. *Briefe (B)*, vol. 7, p. 9.

4. *B*, vol. 7, pp. 50–51.

5. *B*, vol. 7, p. 76; vol. 8, p. 34.

6. *B*, vol. 8, p. 515; Christopher Middleton, ed. and trans., *Selected Letters of Friedrich Nietzsche* (Chicago, 1969), p. 334.

7. *B*, vol. 8, p. 374; Middleton, p. 304.

8. *Briefe (B)*, vol. 6, p. 466; see also vol. 6, p. 474.

9. *B*, vol. 7, p. 33.

10. *B*, vol. 7, p. 9. 11. *B*, vol. 6, p. 455.

12. *B*, vol. 7, p. 46; see also vol. 7, p. 74.

13. See David Farrell Krell, *Postponements: Women, Sensuality and Death in Nietzsche* (Bloomington, Ind., 1986).

14. Two exceptions are Harold Alderman, *Nietzsche's Gift* (Athens, Ohio, 1977) and James Ogilvy, *Many-Dimensional Man* (New York, 1977); see also my account in *Nietzschean Narratives* (Bloomington, Ind., 1989).

15. Michel Serres, *The Parasite*, trans. Lawrence Schehr (Baltimore, 1982), pp. 8–9.

16. See David Farrell Krell, "Daimon Life, Nearness and Abyss: An Introduction to Za-ology," *Research in Phenomenology* (1989): 23–53.

17. Jung's comment on this passage in his lectures on *Zarathustra* suggests some connections between these animal noises and pagan mysteries: "in the mystery cults around Mithras and Bacchus and such pagan syncretistic gods, they imitated on certain occasions the voices of the symbolic animals they represented, roaring like lions or bulls, for instance"; *Nietzsche's Zarathustra*, ed. James L. Jarrett (Princeton, N.J., 1988), p. 35.

18. Serres, *The Parasite*, pp. 3–8.

19. Ibid., *The Parasite*, p. 7.

20. See Rudolf Wittkower, "Eagle and Serpent" in *Allegory and the Migration of Symbols* (London, 1977), pp. 15–44.

21. Serres argues that too much has been made of the supposition that early humans for a long period of time were predominantly hunters. The suggestion is that animals and humans resort to predatory activity only when parasitism is not possible: "the cat lets the mice go if there is cheese left for him. He becomes a predator only if he can no longer parasite someone...preying and hunting need more finesse than sponging. Thus the latter is more probable...hunting...is only the starved distance from parasitism," *The Parasite*, p. 165.

22. Diogenes Laertius, *Lives of the Eminent Philosophies*, trans. R. D. Hicks (Cambridge, 1925), vol. 5, p. 22; cf. Aristotle, *Nicomachean Ethics* 1171a15–17 and *Eudemian Ethics*, 1245b20. On the philosophical thematics of friendship, with reference to Aristotle, Nietzsche, and others, see Jacques Derrida "The Politics of Friendship," *Journal of Philosophy* (1988): 632–644.

23. See also my discussion in *Nietzschean Narratives*, Chapter 4 "Festival, Carnival and Parody," pp. 97–123. That analysis emphasizes the carnivalesque affiliations of *Zarathustra* IV and Nietzsche's use of a certain literary tradition, roughly equivalent to the one mapped in Bakhtin's *Rabelais and His World*. Although still endorsing such a reading, my analysis here in terms of the logic of the parasite is meant to stress a more general structure than is associated with the episodic (or seasonal) occurrence of carnival. I take Nietzsche's repeated insistence in his letters that *Zarathustra* is not to be understood as "literature" as consistent with the attempt to read the text in terms of those general structures of parasitism—dependency, transitivity, noise, and interruption—discussed earlier.

24. Jacques Derrida, *Spurs*, trans. Barbara Harlow (Chicago, 1979), p. 43; and see *The Ear of the Other*, trans. Avital Ronell (New York, 1985).

25. Serres, *The Parasite*, pp. 188–189. 26. I have taken the liberty of paraphasing or parasiting a few lines from my earlier book, *Nietzschean Narratives*, p. 109.

27. Martin Heidegger, *Nietzsche*, trans. David Farrell Krell, especially volume 1: *The Will to Power as Art* (New York, 1979), pp. 151–161, 200–210.

28. Emerson, *Essays and Lectures* (New York, 1983), (pp. 295–296.

29. Bakhtin writes: "The feast of fools is one of the most colorful and genuine expressions of medieval festive laughter near the precincts of the church. Another of its expressions is the 'feast of the ass' commemorating Mary's flight to Egypt with the infant Jesus. The center of this feast is neither Mary nor Jesus, although a young girl with an infant takes part in it. The central protagonist is the ass and its braying. Special 'asinine masses' were celebrated. An *officium* of this mass composed by the austere churchman Pierre Corbeille has been preserved. Each part of the mass was accompanied by the comic braying, 'hinham!' At the end of the service, instead of the usual blessing, *The priest repeated the braying three times*, and the final Amen was replaced by the same cry. The ass is one of the most ancient and lasting symbols of the material bodily lower stratum, which at the same time degrades and regenerates. It is sufficient to recall Apuleius' 'Golden Ass,' the widespread ass-mimes of antiquity, and finally the image of the ass as the symbol of the bodily lower stratum in the legends of Francis of Assisi. The 'feast of the ass' is one of the oldest variants of this theme." *Rabelais and His World*, p. 78.

30. Serres, *The Parasite*, p. 168.

31. Cf. Jacques Derrida, *Speech and Phenomena* trans. David Allison (Evanston, Ill., 1973); and *Of Grammatology*, trans. Gayatri C. Spivak (Baltimore, 1976).

32. See Nietzsche, *On the Genealogy of Morals* and *Ecce Homo*, trans. Walter Kaufmann (New York, 1969), p. 295, n. 1.

33. Serres, *The Parasite*, p. 13.

Alcyone's Song: The Halcyon Tone

Looking back at *Thus Spoke Zarathustra* three or four years later in *Ecce Homo* and looking forward to readers, readers who would share his sense that his work divides the history of humankind into two parts, Nietzsche wanted to say something about listening. He was concerned that this book not be heard in the wrong way; but hearing must be difficult and demanding in the case of a book that embodies, mimes or parodies such an extraordinary range of voices, noise, and music:

> Here no "prophet" is speaking, none of those gruesome hybrids of sickness and will to power whom people call founders of religions. Above all, one must *hear* aright the tone that comes from this mouth, the halcyon tone, lest one should do wretched injustice to the meaning of its wisdom. (*EH*, 219; *6*, 259)

And at that point Nietzsche cites two passages from the second part of *Zarathustra* and comments "It is no fanatic that speaks here..." What is the halcyon tone that speaks in *Zarathustra*? Most readers will know what the *Oxford English Dictionary* (or some similar source) would tell them, namely that *halcyon* means "calm, quiet, peaceful, undisturbed" and that the adjective usually qualifies *days*. And although this has become a relatively common word recently, it was not always so. German lexicons note that although the adjective *halkyonisch* had some play in eighteenth century writers such as Wieland, it fell into disuse until revived by Nietzsche.[1] We might observe now that since, even for Wieland, this was a *Fremdwort*, foreign or strange word, and that Nietzsche's sources are Greek and Latin, halcyon (*halkyonisch*) is not a German word. This may be the reason why philosophers like Heidegger have not attended to it. In fact, as we shall see, the halcyon, in one of its significant Nietzschean uses, is the antithesis of the German.

The passages that Nietzsche cites to confirm the halcyon tone exhibit a certain pacific mood, (a *Stimmung*, let us say,) that one can hear, at least occasionally in *Zarathustra:* "It is the stillest words that bring on the storm. Thoughts that come on dove's feet guide the world" (Z, 168; 4, 189). And:

> The figs are falling from the trees; they are good and sweet; and as they fall their ripe skin bursts, I am a north wind to ripe figs.
>
> Thus, like figs, these teachings fall to you my friends: now consume their juice and their sweet meat. It is fall around us, and pure sky and afternoon. (Z, 109; 4, 109)

Surely it is of interest that Nietzsche, in insisting on our hearing *Zarathustra's* halcyon tone, refers us to the sonorous, voiced, musical qualities of the text. Is there then a single voice or tone underlying the babble and Babel of tongues, the almost impossible opera whose libretto is *Zarathustra* IV? The first text that Nietzsche cites as a reminder of the halcyon tone is from "The Stillest Hour," an uncanny silent dialogue in which the stillest hour speaks to Zarathustra without voice. What can be the tone of a voiceless voice?

Before going further let's note that the calm and richness suggested by "dove's feet" and the "pure sky and afternoon" of fall are counterposed to the storm that the stillest words will bring on and the north wind that shakes the fig trees. Birds, storms, ripeness—these may have something to do with the halcyon and its tone. And the halcyon is also, among other things, a bird, the kingfisher or *Eisvogel* whose nesting and hatching of eggs is associated with the opposition of calm peaceful seas to wind and storm. Might the halcyon tone be the cry of that bird? A complex question to which we shall return, but it raises the preliminary question, returning to Nietzsche's protocol of hearing and reading: just *whose* mouth is "this mouth" that gives voice to the halcyon tone? One might suppose that the voice is Zarathustra's, a supposition that could be reinforced by the fact that the second passage cited is spoken by him; they are not the words of the narrator nor of other persons of the story. The first words are those of "the stillest hour," which could be understood as one of Zarathustra's voices. Yet a few lines earlier Nietzsche describes the text, *Thus Spoke Zarathustra* in this way: "This book, with a *voice* bridging centuries, is not only the highest book there is." Does that settle the question or simply introduce more possible owners of the voice? We've already identified some of the possible speakers (or perhaps singers), for Nietzsche doesn't say in what mode this tone comes from "this mouth": the character Zarathustra, Nietzsche as an author, the halcyon bird, the book or text of *Zarathustra*. So many voices, so many styles. In *Ecce Homo*, after declaring "I come from heights that no bird ever reached in its flight, I know abysses into which no foot ever strayed," Nietzsche claims that he has "the most multifarious art of style that has ever been at the disposal of one man" (*EH,265; 6,* 304). The list of possible voices could be complicated if we recall that the halcyon, as inscribed in the texts and myths of the ancient world, is the bird into which Alcyone was transformed, when her husband Ceyx was also metamorphosed into a bird.[2] As so often in Nietzsche a name begins to appear where we thought that we had heard an adjective or a common noun. This antonomasia can be detected throughout Nietzsche's texts; and the fascination with what the *Genealogy of Morals* calls "the sovereign right of giving names" also surfaces in the declaration of January 1889, "I am all the *names* of history" and in Nietzsche's genealogical meditations on his "Polish" ancestry in *Ecce Homo*.

But what's in a name? Are we beginning to make too much of a word? Remember that *Ecce Homo* is the book in which, again in his account of *Thus Spoke Zarathustra*, Nietzsche attempts to enlist us in a labyrinthine quest for the meaning of the name Ariadne. He inscribes the halcyon twice more in that meditation on *Zarathustra* that tempts and seduces us with the figure of Ariadne, as if to reinforce the protocol already cited: "The halcyon, the light feet, the omnipresence of malice and exuberance, and whatever else is typical of the type of Zarathustra—none of this has ever before been dreamed as essential to greatness" (*EH*, 305; *6*, 344). Here again the invocation of the halcyon is immediately followed by a quotation from Zarathustra. This time it is the passage from "On Old and New Tablets," section 19. But in the version given in *Ecce Homo*, two phrases are left out without any indication of the omission. I italicize the omitted words:

> The soul that has the longest ladder and reaches down deepest, *how should the most parasites not sit on that?*
> The soul that loves itself most, in which all things have their sweep and countersweep and ebb and flow *oh, how should the highest soul not have the worst parasites?*

If Nietzsche's text is to be halcyon then it may need to exclude the parasites. But then this text is caught up in the same rhythm of inclusion and exclusion, inside and outside, that characterized the parasitic itself. Eventually we will need to ask whether the halcyon can maintain the light-hearted purity with which it is presented here. In a draft for the chapter "Why I Am a Destiny" Nietzsche calls himself a halcyon figure (the only time he does so): "Have I been understood? He who enlightens about morality is a *force majeure*, a destiny—This shouldn't prevent me from being the most cheerful man, from being a halcyon figure (*ein Halkyonier*), and I even have a right to that" (*14*, 512). In the published text he says, recounting the inspired composition of *Zarathustra*, that it was "under the halcyon sky of Nizza, which then shone into my life for the first time, I found *Zarathustra* III—and was finished" (*EH*, 302; *6*, 341).

But what is the halcyon tone? Perhaps we need to begin to look into the story of Alcyone, because so many of Nietzsche's invocations of the halcyon have to do with wind, storm, sea birds, sky, and intimate productivity (pregnancy or egg hatching) that are parts of that myth. Let's not decide prematurely that in hearing this story (or a few of its versions) that we are decoding the secret of Nietzsche, one that he knows but has artfully concealed, or that we are producing a psychoanalysis that he could not have provided for himself, or that we are revealing his thought to be a new kind of mythology as Ernst Bertram did in his once very influential *Nietzsche: Versuch einer Mythologie*.[3] All these strategies are both valuable and questionable and perhaps we can use our attempt to articulate the halcyon as a way of interrogating the uncanny attractions of such ways of reading.

The fullest and most familiar account of Alcyone is found in Ovid, one of Nietzsche's favorite poets, and one from whom he adopts the motto *"nitimur in vetitum"* ("we seek the forbidden") in the Preface to *Ecce Homo* (it also is cited in *BGE* 227; 5, 162). It's a story from the *Metamorphoses*, so it's a tale of *Verwandlung*. More specifically it has to do with a transformation from human to animal form (to bird form) with a marine setting. As Ovid tells the story, Alcyone was the loving wife of Keyx, son of Lucifer and king of Trochis. We must recall Ovid's version slowly and carefully, for there's a story within the story. Peleus, Achilles' father, was driven into exile after killing his own brother; he took refuge with Keyx at a time when the latter was mourning the death of *his* brother Daedalion. That brother had been transformed by Apollo into a particularly savage bird of prey, after attempting suicide by throwing himself from Mount Parnassus. The further back we go with these bird stories the more sex and death we find. For Daedalion's suicide was occasioned by Diana's murder of his daughter Chione. Chione had the good fortune and the misfortune to be so beautiful that both Mercury (or Hermes) and Apollo made love to her in the same day. (Mercury, cunning and quick as ever, got to her first.) So she boasted of her beauty and the twins she bore, foolishly claiming to be more beautiful than Diana, who responded with one of her arrows. Now as soon as Keyx has told Peleus *that* story, Peleus learns that a supernatural wolf has been killing the cattle and men that he's brought with him into his exile in Trochis. Distraught on account of all these disasters, Keyx resolves to take a long sea journey to consult an oracle (men think that there are answers to the questions posed by suffering). Alcyone's story, in a more limited sense, begins at this point and Ovid draws it out; it is the longest episode in his book of changes. Alcyone begs Keyx not to set sail because she's terrified of the sea; or at least to take her along if he must go. But he leaves alone and the storm that we have all been expecting breaks out; for Ovid it's a great set piece, a storm to end all storms. Alcyone is ignorant of what's happened and for many days she expects his return. But Juno, to whom she's praying for Keyx's safety, takes pity on her and sends a message through a complex route. She dispatches Iris, her messenger, to Sleep with the request that he send Keyx's image to Alcyone in a dream. This is an elaborate postal system for sending a death announcement: Juno to Iris to Sleep to Morpheus, who will present himself as Keyx. One doesn't want to be directly associated with bad news. (Iris is a carrier of messages or an interpreter between humans and gods by vocation, having tasks similar to Hermes'; perhaps this complex chain is an indication of what iristics, the feminine alternative to hermeneutics, might be if we introduce our own antonomasia.) The announcement's made, and Alcyone runs distractedly to the shore where she sees Keyx's body floating toward her. Ovid now tells us of her transformation, one with lasting consequences for all those who live or love by the sea:

> "It is he," she said, "he has come back to me."
> She stripped herself, then ran upon a breaker
> That caught the waves, and leaped as if broad wings
> Took her to sea; even her cries were birdlike;
> And as she neared the floating man beneath her,
> She thrust her growing beak between his lips.
> The story is: he raised his face to hers,
> And I half think Keyx did—if he had life.
> The gods changed both to birds, and both were one,
> Though love had given them a strange mutation.
> Today they live and breed upon those waters
> And for a week in winter, Alcyone
> Keeps her brood warm within a floating nest,
> Aeolus stills the winds that shake the waters
> To guard his grandsons on a peaceful sea.[4]

This last part of the story is the explanation of the halcyon days, telling how a woman's name became inscribed in a bird and in the cosmic rhythms of the sea and sky.

The story of Alcyone is inscribed throughout Greek and Latin philosophy, poetry, and natural history. It will become clear, however, that there is no single version of the myth but rather a series of variations that we can suppose the young Nietzsche to have absorbed in his philological labors. From Homer to Ovid, from Aristotle to Plutarch, from Aristophanes to the Byzantine scholiasts on Greek writings, Alcyone or the bird that bears her name flutters through the classical texts. When Nietzsche invokes the halcyon, as he does more and more frequently after writing *Zarathustra*, especially to characterize the tone of his greatest gift, we should be aware of at least part of this vast repertoire that he can draw on.

By the time of the late classical period for which Ovid writes, Alcyone had become an emblem of loving fidelity. In the final volume of his *History of Sexuality*, Michel Foucault has traced the ways in which the sexual ethics of Hellenistic and Roman times came to elevate the status of marriage, seeing it as based on a genuine reciprocity of interests, activities, and conversation. This ideal of companionship is found in the handbooks, medical guides, and compendia of advice by Plutarch, Galen, Seneca, and others.[5] But they also found a literary mythical or psychological expression, even being read into the accounts of natural history we now see as inscribed with ideals of human conduct. Pauly-Wissowa tells us that "The name Alcyone was bound up with the idea of faithful married love"; it is notable that although there is even a fleeting reference in the *Iliad* that can be so construed, these associations of the name become much more pronounced in late Hellenistic and Roman times when writers like Plutarch are searching for mythical and narrative equivalents of their more prosaic handbooks on marriage.[6]

Earlier, even the sober Aristotle reports that the halcyon days occur at the traditional time of the winter solstice, although he notes that they do not *always* happen as expected and he describes the miraculous nest, although he perhaps expresses a certain skepticism in noting that the halcyon (or kingfisher) is "the most rarely seen of all birds."[7] In the otherwise doggedly prosaic *History of Animals* Aristotle quotes four lines of Simonides in explaining the halcyon days.

God lulls for fourteen days the winds to sleep
In winter; and this temperate interlude
Men call the Holy Season, when the deep
Cradles the mother halcyon and her brood.[8]

In the long section devoted to the copulation and propagation
of animals, this is the only topic that elicits a bit of poetry from
Aristotle. This story and the citation of Simonides occur at a
significant juncture in Aristotle's text. He has just finished
describing the ways in which various animals copulate, speci-
fying their organs and positions. But now he turns to the question of the typical or preferred season for sex, because "for each
kind of animal there are definite seasons and ages for copulation." Here the halcyon constitutes an exception, as it does in so
many respects: "With birds the far greater part, as has been
said, pair and breed during the spring and early summer, with
the exception of the halcyon."[9] So the halcyon's mating and
breeding marks something extraordinary with respect to the
calendar; it sets its own time. The nest also is wonderful and
Aristotle reports quite soberly on its construction to explain
how it floats:

> Its nest is like sea-balls, i. e. the things that go by the name
> of sea-foam, only the color is not the same. The color of the
> nest is light red, and the shape is that of the long-necked
> gourd. The nests are larger than the largest sponge,
> though they vary in size; they are roofed over and great
> part of them is solid and great part hollow. If you use a
> sharp knife it is not easy to cut the nest through; but if you
> cut it, and at the same time bruise it with your hand, it will
> soon crumble to pieces, like sea-foam. The opening is
> small, just enough for a tiny entrance, so that even if the
> nest capsizes the sea does not enter in; the hollow chan-
> nels are like those in sponges. It is not known for certain of
> what material the nest is constructed; it is possibly made
> of the backbones of the gar-fish; for the bird lives on fish.[10]

Of the many noteworthy features of this report perhaps the
most noteworthy is the way in which Aristotle produces the

effect of judicious scientific observation by carefully distin-
guishing what is definitely known and what is still to be determined with certainty. However, such an account already was
parodied in the ancient world by Lucian, who in his *True History* has his travelers encounter a gigantic halcyon nest that turns
out to be a floating island of sixty stadia in circumference. But
some of the more prosaic aspects of Aristotle's account are also
questionable; as D'Arcy Thompson points out in *A Glossary of
Greek Birds*, neither of the species of kingfisher known in Greece
can sing, although Aristotle purports to distinguish a singing
and a nonsinging species. With some understatement he comments that "[t]he whole matter is confused and mystical."[11]

The position of the halcyon in Aristotle's biological works
is worth exploring. First it must be remembered that Aristotle,
a physician and close student of animal life, gives a radically
different account of the relation between man and animal than
the Orphics, the Pythagoreans, or Plato and his followers—all
of whose thought, in lending itself to a dualism of soul and
body, tends to lump together all nonhuman animals. Aristotle
not only describes man as the *zoon logon echon*, the animal with
logos, he also is keenly aware of the many differences among
animals. In his biological works he produces a taxonomic
schema in which animals are ranked and differentiated in so far
as they approach the human condition. The halcyon eludes a
number of Aristotle's principles of classification; for example it
is laid down at the beginning of the *History of Animals* that

> of those that live in the water some do so in one way, and
> some in another: that is to say, some live and feed in the
> water, take in and emit water, and cannot live if deprived
> of water, as is the case with the great majority of fishes;
> others get their food and spend their days in the water, but
> do not take in water but air, nor do they bring forth in the
> water.[12]

The anomalies of the halcyon's reproduction makes this species
something of an intermediary case between the birds and the
cetaceans. Some have thought that the halcyon's very name
alkuon is, etymologically, "sea breeding" that is derived from

hals and *kuo* (and in Latin *alcedo*).[13] Not only is the nest itself
wonderful and unlike any other, but there is an extraordinary
connection between the breeding time of the halcyon and the
weather. Now Aristotle's works on animals, it has often been
observed, seem to show an especially sharp eye and preference
for life in and around the sea, and it is supposed that many of
his observations must have been made along the seashore of
Asia Minor, near Lesbos. Although some commentators have
described the *History of Animals* as a collective notebook, con-
taining a disparate group of observations, these sections stand
out for their poetry, both as cited and as implicit in the remarkable story told; if some editorial control was exercised on the
collection one would suppose that there was a philosophical
endorsement for the inclusion of this extraordinary material.[14]

Plutarch provides an epitome of the Hellenistic veneration
for the halcyon in a long encomium in "On the Cleverness of
Animals," calling it "the wisest of sea creatures, the most
beloved of the gods." Because of the halcyon days "there is no
other creature that men love more." In loving this animal are
we loving a woman? Plutarch repeats the story found in
Alcman's poetry about the female's devotion in carrying the
aged male on her back and praises her skill and ingenuity in
building the nest, allowing that "what she contrives and constructs would be hard to believe without ocular evidence." The
account ends on a somewhat mysterious note:

> Now I presume that all of you have seen this nest; as for
> me, since I have often seen and touched it, it comes to my
> mind to chant the words "Once such a thing in Delos near
> Apollo's shrine..."[15]

Like Aristotle, the halcyon moves Plutarch to poetry, or at least
to citation (the line is from the *Odyssey* VI. 162). D'Arcy Thompson, translator of Aristotle's *History of Animals* and author of
the magisterial *Glossary of Greek Birds* remarks "[T]hat there was
some religious mystery associated with the so-called nest is
indicated by the close of Plutarch's description."[16]

But what is the halcyon tone? Is it the sense of great peace
and calm that comes when the seas are suddenly, miraculously

still, and you're hatching your eggs? *Zarathustra* and Nietzsche's other writings are replete with images of the sea and of
pregnancy; in fact we've already cited Nietzsche's confession
that he carried *Zarathustra* to term under the "halcyon skies" of
Nizza, and we might note that these were the halcyon skies of
January 1884, that is, just after the winter solstice. The halcyon
days make their appearance in a passage of Emerson that
young Nietzsche remarked in a letter of 1866 to Carl Gersdorff;
Nietzsche's letter is often cited as evidence of his early and
intense interest in the American writer.

> Dear friend,
> Occasionally there come hours of quiet contemplation,
> where one stand beyond one's life in mixed joy and sor-
> row, as in those beautiful summer days, which lie broad
> and comfortable over the hills, as Emerson describes them
> so splendidly: then nature becomes complete, as he says,
> and so do we: then we are free of the captivity of the will,
> which is always awake, then are we a pure intuitive eye,
> devoid of interest. (April 7, 1866; *Briefe*, vol. 2: 119–120)

The attempt to link Emerson and Schopenhauer is somewhat
tendentious. Emerson had written:

> There are days which occur in this climate, at almost any
> season of the year, wherein the world reaches its perfec-
> tion.... These halcyons may be looked for with a little
> more assurance in that pure October weather, which we
> distinguish by the name of the Indian Summer.[17]

Here we see how in relatively recent discourse the halcyon
days are not necessarily fixed at a specific point in the calendar.
    Nevertheless, the story as the ancients told it is clearly
cyclical and calendrical; modern commentators have suggested
that it has important sidereal and solar dimensions. It is possible to imagine that these could appeal to the philosopher of
eternal recurrence. D'Arcy Thompson, who favors astronomical
explanations of the legends associated with birds proposes that
the story is connected with the Pleiades, in which Alcyone is

the principal star; the rising and setting of the Pleiades would then be identified as the flight or nestings of the bird.[18] As a late Victorian biologist, Thompson took an interest in interpreting myth as proto-science. A more recent study by a classicist begins from the standpoint of comparative mythology, noting the prevalence of stories throughout the world of humans changed into birds and of birds having a magical power over the weather. Charles K. Gresseth challenges Thompson's sidereal reading by pointing out that the Pleiades are connected with the spring and autumn equinoxes rather than with the winter solstice. His solar explication of the myth, on the surface, is a more Nietzschean one:

> in comparative myth the sun is frequently symbolized as a bird; further, that, as in the case of the phoenix, birds in myth often renew themselves. In the myth of Alcyone these motifs were combined to form a story of the rebirth of the sun at the time of the winter solstice.[19]

On this interpretation the legend of the female carrying the aged male would be part of a truncated story of rebirth, and the miraculous nest would be the sun's launching pad. Birds and the sun are invoked throughout *Zarathustra*, and one can see how the halcyon tone could be construed in terms of a solar story of rebirth that would function as a mythical and textual unconscious of the alternation of noon, midnight, and dawn. And, as we shall see soon, Nietzsche seems to have had a special feeling for the time of the winter solstice, which he sometimes baptizes as Sanctus Januarius and which was the recurring time of some of his greatest exaltations as well as of his official entry into madness.

But perhaps we need to make a distinction between halcyon days (and their associated seas and skies) and a halcyon *tone* that comes from the mouth (whose mouth?). If the halcyon tone is the cry of the halcyon then the myth as we have it so far tells us two very interesting things: that the cry is a lament, a *Klage*, and that it is the cry of a woman or a woman transformed into a bird, Alcyone. The ancients were intrigued by two things about the behavior of the halcyon, its beautiful, seductive, sorrowful cry (which could be heard by anyone) and its power to build a floating nest (which was generally believed although few claimed to have seen it, a notable exception being Plutarch in "On the Cleverness of Animals"). As Norman Douglas points out, the poems of the *Greek Anthology,* in which the halcyon figures frequently sometimes present the cry as shrill and sometimes as of a mournful beauty. And he suggests that these descriptions are not as inconsistent as they might appear at first:

> There is doubtless a difference between shrillness and the plaintive mournfulness attributed to the halcyon, but it may be observed that Mediterranean people are apt to mourn in quite a shrill fashion. Oppian says that the halcyon ends its song by crying out its former human name—Ceyx! Ceyx!—which sounds rather shrill than otherwise.[20]

Among the dialogues attributed to Lucian is one called *Halcyon* that now is generally thought to be spurious. It is a conversation between Socrates and Chairephon that opens with Socrates being asked about a hauntingly beautiful, mournful song: "What is the cry, Socrates, that comes to us from the distant breakers on the headland yonder? How sweet it sounds! What creature has such a note as that? Surely, the water-fowl are voiceless."[21] Socrates answers that it's indeed not a water fowl, but a sea bird, that is one that ordinarily lives further out with little need for the security of land, and that it is "full of plaints and tears," which he explains by telling a brief version of the story we have already cited. (We could compare this beginning of the pseudo-Lucianic *Halcyon* with *The Gay Science,* no. 60, which discuss both the silent woman who performs her action at a distance by appearing to a man as a sailing ship at sea., and no. 70, which explores the powerful effect of a certain kind of female voice; both are analyzed by Derrida in *Spurs.*) This is one "halcyon tone," and it can perhaps be heard in some of the *Klagen* in *Zarathustra:* think of "The Night Song," "The Grave Song" or the *Zauberer's* first song that reappears later (the *gender* of its singer metamorphosed) as the *Klage der Ariadne.*

But surely, we're tempted to say, all of *Zarathustra* is not a *Klage;* perhaps both the *Klage* and expressions of great good cheer more conventionally called *halcyon* are aspects of a cycle of joy and woe, an affirmation of life that can transform suffering into celebration and bring pregnancy out of death. And what of the mouth that utters the halcyon tone? Is the mouth of *Thus Spoke Zarathustra* the mouth of a woman? That would require a subtle ear indeed to discern, but Nietzsche always seeks the smallest, most refined and subtlest ears. In Ovid's *Metamorphoses* one of the chain of stories in Book XI, leading to the narrative of Keyx and Alcyone, tells what happens to Midas after he was freed from the self-inflicted curse of the golden touch. He became a follower of Pan, and along with some uncouth female Pan groupies, thought the music of his pipes was unsurpassed, in fact superior to Apollo's. So a competition was held in which the barbarism of Midas' taste became evident; the gods recognized this by transforming his ears into ass's ears.[22] The competition of singers and the fine judgment required in the ear of the listener is both thematized in Nietzsche (in *Zarathustra* IV, notably, in another song competition) and becomes a dimension of his relation with his reader, whom he begs not to confuse one tone, one voice with another. At the ass festival the ass's ears have all the subtlety of his hee-haw. Remember that in one of the notes published in *The Will to Power* Nietzsche asks, "now that God is dead, who is speaking?" (*WP,* 275). This question clearly can be directed toward the Nietzschean text, too; and we can ask what gender speaks, sings, gurgles, raves or poetizes. There are no women at Zarathustra's party where the midnight song is sung, but that did not prevent Gustav Mahler from making the singer of the whispering version in his *Third Symphony* a woman (in contrast to Richard Strauss's more bombastic treatment of the same section in his tone poem). Nietzsche liked hearing a woman read the songs from *Zarathustra,* especially those of a melancholy or sorrowful tone. Resa von Schirnhofer recalls that Nietzsche had her read the "Night Song," the "Dancing Song," the "Midnight Song," the "Grave Song," and the "Seven Seals." She remembers that she read hesitantly at first but was then overcome herself with the beauty of these songs; so the halcyon voice is autoaffected, the halcyon can hear herself.[23] Meta von

Salis-Marschlins met Nietzsche on July 14, 1884; in her recollection of that and subsequent meetings she assigns the halcyon position to him: "Halcyon and tranquil as he characteristically called himself, the times we were together were halcyon for me, suited to spreading a golden glimmer over the rest of my life."[24]

The halcyon story is a love story, celebrated by many of the poets. As early as the *Iliad* where Alcyone is (it seems) another name for Kleopatra, the devoted wife of Meleager, the name appears to take on the meaning of faithful married love. There is a legend, as in these lines of Alcman, that the young females carry the aged males on their backs:

> O maidens of honey voice so loved and
> dear, my limbs can carry me no more.
> Would O would God I were but a
> ceryl, such as flies fearless of
> heart with the halcyons over the
> bloom of the wave, the spring's own
> bird that is purple as the sea![25]

It is in retrospect from the standpoint of *Ecce Homo* that Nietzsche describes *Zarathustra* in terms of halcyon tones and skies. So we will want to ask what it is about this later perspective that leads him to see and hear his "greatest gift" in this way. But we also should note a number of plans and sketches of 1885–1887 in which the halcyon theme appears. In one group of entries, which according to Colli and Montinari's dating of the notebooks may themselves have been written during the halcyon days of the winter solstice, there is first what seems to be a sketch of a poem or poems with the title *"Halkyonische Reden"* and the apparent subtitle "Caesar among Pirates." Perhaps the "Halcyon Discourses" are Caesar's; Plutarch, in his *Lives of the Illustrious Greeks and Romans* says that when Caesar was seized by pirates and waiting to be ransomed, he amused himself by composing songs and speeches that he insisted on singing and reciting to his captors. These would be cheery songs at sea by one of history's strongest men, one of Nietzsche's favorites.[26] The sketch contains twenty-three lines that could suggest either the first lines or titles of poems (or sections of a narrative), such as:

Frauen-Tanz, Thorheit, kleine Schmuckkasten
der Versucher.
Vom Geblüt.
Die Maske.
(Women's dance, foolishness, little jewelry-cases
the tempter.
of descent
the masks)

And immediately following there are what appear to be two
titles of planned works: *Halkyonische Lieder* and *Ariadne* (12, 61).
Ariadne is inscribed next to the songs of Alcyone, as she is in
Ecce Homo; these are the two women Nietzsche calls on there to
situate the voice and the sense of *Zarathustra.* Another entry
from a notebook of 1885 announces

Halkyonische Zwischenreden
Zur Erholung von "Also Sprach Zarathustra"
  seiner Freunden geweiht
    von
  Friedrich Nietzsche
(Halcyon Interludes
  Toward Rest/Recovery from *Thus Spoke Zarathustra*
    dedicated to his friends). (12, 68)

Here *Zarathustra* seems to be the storm that requires calm seas
and peaceful skies for the recovery of the author. And one of
the possible subtitles that Nietzsche sketched for *Beyond Good
and Evil* is

Allerhand Nachdenkliches
  für halkyonische Geister (12, 77)
  (Thoughts of All Sorts
  for Halcyon Spirits)

Note that the halcyon function circulates here from the genre to
the singer of the songs to the intended readers of a formally
more prosaic book. Is *Zarathustra* halcyon or is it the storm that
requires a halcyon recovery? The halcyon appears frequently in

Beyond Good and Evil, notably in the penultimate aphorism, again in conjunction with Ariadne, as Dionysus the tempter god is said to "smile his halcyon smile," this just after he has mused on how man might be made "stronger, more evil, more profound and more beautiful" (*BGE*, 295). Dionysus is a sexually ambiguous, androgynous, polymorphic god. His halcyon smile is more than the expression of a great contentment; like everything else about this god it is double or many sided and masklike. Does his halcyon smile at this point evoke the woman whose sorrow is turned into joy, whose drowning is metamorphosed into the power of flight? In the notebooks that precede *Beyond Good and Evil* is a passage that the editors conjecture is a fragment of poetry in which the "halcyon smile" appears. It is apparently a woman who speaks:

> The orgiastic soul—
> I've seen him: at least his eyes—
> now they are deep and quiet, now
> green and lustful
> (*schlüpfrig*) honey-eyes
>   his halcyon smile
>   the sky appeared bloody and fierce. (12, 47)

Here a woman sees the halcyon smile (of Dionysus?) as a sexual invitation.

An earlier form returns in another title in a notebook of 1887:

> *Halkyonia*
> *Nachmittage eines Glucklichen* (12, 453)
>   (Halcyonics
> Afternoons of a Happy Man)

These are attractive book titles and it would be a most seductive temptation to devote a fraction of the energy toward reconstructing and commenting on one of them that has been lavished on that rather prosaic and speculative collection, *The Will to Power*.[27] Even in that mixed assemblage of jottings is a note that begins by exclaiming "—And how many new gods are still possible!" Nietzsche answers the challenge: "I should not doubt that there are many kinds of gods—There are some one cannot imagine without a certain halcyon and frivolous quality in their make-up—" (*WP*, 1038). Birds, men, music, gods—the halcyon circulates (or flies) among these.

In *Ecce Homo* Nietzsche will invoke the halcyon three times, each time in connection with *Zarathustra*. He wants to reinforce the connection between his "greatest gift," its tonality, and its weather. The section that Nietzsche devotes to *Zarathustra* can be read rather rigorously in the light of the halcyonic mythemes: weather, storm, pregnancy, music, voice. The entire narrative of *Zarathustra* is the story of Nietzsche's pregnancy. First it is important to fix the date of conception. Was it August 1881 when the *Grundconception* came to him or the spring of 1881 when "I discovered together with my maestro and friend Peter Gast, that the phoenix of music flew past us with lighter and more brilliant feathers than it had ever displayed before" (*EH*, 295; 6, 335).

There is some question then about both the time and the agency of Nietzsche's insemination. Was the seed contained in the thought of eternal recurrence or in the phoenix of music? The phoenix shares many of the remarkable characteristics of the halcyon, being involved in a miraculous cycle of death and rebirth; both phoenix and halcyon have been taken to be closely related to the cycle of the solar year.[28] Nietzsche, like some other mothers, is a bit uncertain just how things got started; it could have been that idea that just came to him or a musical bird; in any case, there is something mysterious, certainly something airy, perhaps birdlike about the moment of conception. We are reminded of the transformations of the Olympians in their amours. All in all, Nietzsche seems to think the father was that amazing musical phoenix of brilliant plumage and flickering feathers. And like some other mothers, this one finds it very significant that parturition occurs in sequence with other consequential events:

> But if I reckon forward from that day [when "the phoenix of music flew past us"] to the sudden birth (*Niederkunft*) that occurred in February 1883 under the most improbable

circumstances—the *finale* from which I have quoted a few
sentences in the Preface was finished exactly in that sacred
hour in which Richard Wagner died in Venice—we get
eighteen months for the pregnancy. This figure of precisely
eighteen months might suggest, at least to Buddhists that I
am really a female elephant. (*EH*, 295; *Z*, 335–336)

By means of a learned joke about the elephant's period of
gestation, Nietzsche reinforces both his presentation of himself
as fecund and female ("the secret of my existence is that I am
alive as my mother...") and his concern with the calendar. In
this musical passage about music, Nietzsche is associating the
thought of the *Wiederkunft* with his own *Niederkunft*. During
this pregnancy the expectant mother (so the story in *Ecce Homo*
goes) was generally quiet, but merely gave some signs of the
remarkable birth that was to come. In this interval she produced the *"gaya scienza"* (in Italian, a musical language) that
"contains a hundred signs of the proximity of something
incomparable."[29] And within this story of pregnancy, Nietzsche
tells another story of artistic creation (in much greater detail
than that in which he alludes to *The Gay Science*), this one, again
like *Zarathustra*, having a pair of parents. This story, which
we've already encountered, should be reread with some care:

> Something else also belongs to this interval: that *Hymn to
> Life* (for mixed choir and orchestra) whose score was pub-
> lished two years ago by E. W. Fritzsch in Leipzig—a
> scarcely trivial symptom of my condition (*Zustand*) during
> that year when the Yes-saying pathos *par excellence*, which
> I call the tragic pathos, was alive in me to the highest
> degree. The time will come when it will be sung in my
> memory.

This symptom of Nietzsche's delicate condition was to be sung
by a *mixed* chorus—male and female—unlike, so it seems, the
all too male cast of *Zarathustra*. It marks a certain time and (he
promises us) it will come to mark *his* time. Male and female
voices, singing together, will celebrate the memory of Friedrich
Nietzsche. As in the case of *Zarathustra* itself, Nietzsche feels a

need to reveal the true parentage of this song. (*Ecce Homo* shows an obsessive concern with getting the genealogies right):

> The text, to say this expressly because a misunderstanding has gained currency, is not by me: it is the amazing inspiration of a young Russian woman who was my friend at that time (*Mit der ich damals befreundet war*), Fraulein Lou von Salomé. Whoever can find any meaning at all in the last words of this poem will guess why I preferred and admired it: they attain greatness. Pain is *not* considered an objection to life: "If you have no more happiness to give me, well then! *you still have suffering.*" Perhaps my music, too, attains greatness at this point. (Last note of the A-clarinet, c flat, not c: misprint.) (*EH*, 296–297; 6, 336)

The text was an inspiration, certainly Lou Salomé's, but was it also the inspiration of the whole composition? The language hints at this but does not confirm it. If so, Lou would be the father of the work and Nietzsche would have had multiple pregnancies in the same period of time. Yet one of the constants of Nietzsche's musical aesthetics is that words ought not to determine music. Even when Wagner is no longer praised, this principle of his criticism of the opera is retained. Birth and pain, male and female—Nietzsche wants to make sure that we do not *misunderstand* how these are associated with the genesis of *Zarathustra*. Aren't these constituents or presuppositions of the halcyon tone that we must "*hear* right" if we are not to do "wretched injustice to the meaning of its wisdom"?

The rest of this bird and birth story deals with inspiration, health, illness, recovery, weather, places, tones, and the uniqueness of *Zarathustra*. All the aspects of composition are mapped onto the ornithological or the meteorological. Climbing, for example, is the ascent to a nest, and so takes on the character of bird's flight despite the human effort it involves:

> Many concealed spots and heights in the landscape around Nizza are hallowed for me by unforgettable moments; that decisive passage which bears the title "On Old and New Tablets" was composed on the most onerous

ascent to the marvelous Moorish eyrie (*Felsenneste:* a nest in the cliffs), Eza—the suppleness of my muscles has always been greatest when my creative energies were flowing most abundantly. (*EH*, 302; *6*, 347)

The bird in this eyrie high up in the cliffs, let's recall, is concerned to escape from parasites and their nauseous nests; at the same time it's acknowledged that the most spacious souls attract the most parasites ("On Old and New Tablets" 19: *Z*, 225; *4*, 261).

To be inspired is to be taken over (as by a god, under the cloak of invisibility): "A rapture whose tremendous tension occasionally discharges itself in a flood of tears—now the pace quickens involuntarily, now it becomes slow" (*EH*, 300; *6*, 339). He was ill; he recovered. Fate brought him back to Rome and to the melancholy that was required for the composition of the "Night Song." "The next winter, under the halcyon sky of Nizza, which then shone into my life for the first time, I found *Zarathustra* III—and was finished. Scarcely a year for the whole of it" (*EH*, 302; *6*, 341) Halcyon at the finish. Just the right skies, the skies of Nice, known in Italian as Nizza, and so marked for this adept at finding musical coincidences, by a version of his/her name. Nice is on the Mediterranean, the sea of the halcyon. So Nice/Nizza/Nietzsche is the site of the birth of the last of the triplets. There are two names in this birth announcement, Alcyone's and Nietzsche's, each transfigured. The delivery lasted ten days, just about the time specified by the ancient authorities. This story, or myth, of *Zarathustra's* composition requires some simplifications, some operatic fierceness with the facts. We know that Nietzsche accumulated notes and drafts for the four parts of *Zarathustra* almost continuously; the period of pregnancy was a busy time. And we know that there is something suspicious about the repeated insistence that Part III was the completion of the "whole." Even without the evidence of the now published Part IV, a careful reader of *Ecce Homo* might note an allusion to an episode in Zarathustra's story that does not find its way into Parts I–III. In "Why I am so Wise" Nietzsche writes: "The overcoming of pity I count among the *noble* virtues: as 'Zarathustra's temptation' I created a situation (*einen Fall gedichtet*) in which a great cry of distress reaches him" (*EH*, 228; *6*, 270).

One might wonder, Is the halcyon myth operative not only in *Zarathustra,* as Nietzsche suggests, but also in this story of an incomparable pregnancy and birth? In setting the record straight Nietzsche manages to inscribe all the essential elements of Alcyone's story, down to her name, which recurs when Nietzsche tries to say something of what is unique, almost unnamable, about the figure whom his letters call "my son Zarathustra":

> Here man has been overcome at every moment; the concept of the *Übermensch* has here become the greatest reality—whatever was so far considered great in man lies beneath him at an infinite distance. The halcyon, the light feet, the onmipresence of malice and exuberance, and whatever else is typical of the type of Zarathustra—none of this has ever before been dreamed of as essential to greatness. Precisely in this width of space and this accessibility for what is contradictory, Zarathustra experiences himself as the *supreme type of all beings.* (EH, 305; 6, 344)

All of this, Nietzsche adds, is not to be understood by metaphor, but as the concept of Dionysus himself. Dionysus, we recall, has a halcyon smile.

Nietzsche tells us that the halcyon is inscribed in *Zarathustra,* an inscription that (we will confirm) has something to do with the width of space. Certainly there is no shortage of birds there, although many have wondered why they were flitting through these heavy pages (heavy if one doesn't attend to the halcyon tone). One bird of special interest occurs in Zarathustra's discussion of the nameability of virtue in "Of Joys and Passions." The problem that provokes this talk is the all too human desire to find common names for our virtues, to identify our courage or our charity, for example. But in so identifying them we see nothing more in them than what is commonly or ordinarily said; our own specific gift is occluded because we find no name for it.

> "My brother, if you have a virtue and it is your own virtue, you have it in common with no one.
>
> To be sure, you want to call it by a name and caress it; you want to pull its ears and amuse yourself with it.

And behold! Now you have its name in common with the people and have become of the people and the herd with your virtue!

You would do better to say 'Unutterable and nameless is that which torments and delights my soul and is also the hunger of my belly.'" (Z, 63; 4, 42)

If there is a virtue that is Zarathustra's, it is the gift-giving virtue he praises when his disciples present him, later, with a gift. It is that process of articulating and naming the gift-giving virtue that, even later, he will characterize as "naming the unnamable." So we have to acknowledge that, although it is best not to name one's virtue and so risk degrading it by forcing it within the moral language of the people and the herd, there are times when this prohibition may be transgressed and a name may be given to the unnamable. We already have suggested some of the ways in which *die schenkende Tugend* must be unnamable from the perspective of the moral economy of the nation, private property, and Christianity, which constitute the moral language of modernity. Yet, even here, before his discourse on the gift-giving virtue in which Zarathustra exercises the sovereign right of giving names, there already is a kind of mininarrative in which he indicates what it means to have one's own virtue:

"It is an earthly virtue that I love: there is little prudence in it, and least of all common wisdom.

"But this bird has built its nest with me: therefore I love and cherish it—now it sits there upon its golden eggs."

Thus should you stammer and praise your virtue. (Z, 64; 4, 42)

The nameless virtue is a bird hatching golden, miraculous eggs; Zarathustra looks forward to the time when these gifts will hatch. This story that connects an as yet nameless virtue with a nesting bird *verges* on naming and so one could say "thus stammered Zarathustra." This is not the only time that Zarathustra identifies himself as a bird or the guardian of a bird, and it is notable that amidst the plethora of animals invoked in

Zarathustra, the bird almost exclusively is the subject of these identifications. To become-animal here is to become-bird. In one case the bird is to be protected by others and fed only the cleanest food, a food quite different from the nasty things that parasites would eat. In "Of the Rabble" (*Vom Gesindel*) the threat of nausea looms once again:

> "But I once asked, and my question almost stifled me: What, does life have *need* of the rabble, too?
>
> Are poisoned wells necessary, and striking fires and dirty dreams and maggots in the bread of life?
>
> Not my hate but my nausea (*Ekel*) hungrily devoured my life! Alas, I often grew weary of the spirit (*Geistes*) when I found the rubble, too, had been gifted with spirit." (Z, 121; 4, 125)

To flee disgust is not only to fly but to become bird:

> "Did my nausea itself create wings and water-divining powers for me? Truly I had to fly to the extremest height to find again the fountain of delight...
>
> We build our nest in the tree Future; eagles shall bring food to us solitaries in their beaks!
>
> Truly, food in which no unclean men could join us!" (Z, 121–122; 4, 125–126)

Earlier Zarathustra was the bird's protector; it was his virtue and yet it might fly away some day. Now he (and his "brothers") become birds protected by other birds. Becoming-bird is a way of evading the danger of nausea; here it means that one will not only eat selectively, like a bird, but have one's food already chosen and preselected by other birds.

In *Ecce Homo* the halcyon is inscribed in Nietzsche's account of the completion of *Zarathustra* with the writing of Part III; and in general the halcyon in his texts calls to mind that which is finished, whole, and self-sufficient. Part III, to the extent that it is a completion (and attempts to bracket or evade the question of the supplemental and the parasitical), has an ending of its own, an end within the end. This end is constituted by the songs Zarathustra sings by himself after the dialogue with his animals in "The Convalescent"; his wrestling with his most abysmal thought there was provoked again by a yawning, looming nausea, and his animals greeted him on his recovery with the choicest food brought by the eagle. These songs, if we follow Nietzsche's protocols in *Ecce Homo*, must be heard with an ear for their halcyon tone. But it is not only the tone that evokes halcyon themes, for birds, sea, sky, and storms appear immediately and figure in the crescendo of "The Seven Seals," which is the last of the songs. In "Of the Great Longing" Zarathustra addresses his soul:

> "With the storm that is called 'spirit' (*Geist*) I blew across your surging sea; I blew all clouds away, I killed even that killer-bird (*Würgerin*) called 'sin.'
>
> Oh my soul, I gave you the right to say no like the storm and to say yes as the open sky says yes: now, silent as light you stand, and you pass through denying storms." (Z, 238; 4, 278)

Spirit (*Geist*) is a storm. The value of this notion in Nietzsche is highly ambiguous. On the one hand spirit is life and vitality, opposed to death, monotony, and small-minded routine. But *Geist* is also the comprehensive concept and emblem of a certain philosophical tradition, notably German, that attempts to evade the material, the bodily, and difference. Even when spirit is praiseworthy it is not inviolable; it certainly is not an eternal value. So in "Of Reading and Writing" Zarathustra can valorize *Geist* in an initial comparison ("Write with blood: and you will discover that blood is spirit") while sensing the possible corruptions of *Geist* ("Another century of readers—and spirit itself will stink"). Here spirit is stormy and confused, like the German weather, both meteorological and cultural, that Nietzsche contrasts with the halcyon element. Storms are fine in so far as they blow away clouds and vapors, clearing the sky for something better. Like the halcyon bird, the soul to whom Nietzsche croons here has an affinity both with the storm (Alcyone is Aeolus' daughter) and with the clear skies and calm seas that follow on them. The attempt to find a nonidealistic, non-Cartesian, even "nonspiritual" sense of spirit here is one that will surface again in the many transformations of the word *Geist* and its derivatives in Heidegger, which Derrida has marked.[30] Heidegger seeks such a nonidealistic, non-metaphysical sense of spirit in Trakl's poetry, where the latter speaks of flame and the animal; but before Heidegger Nietzsche finds spirit in a bird.

"The Seven Seals" alludes to the *Apocalypse* and suggests a certain mystery that might or might not be disclosed. Each of the numbered sections sings of a marriage with eternity and the wedding ring of eternity. These themes are linked directly to the question of pregnancy, specifically male pregnancy: "blessed is he who is thus pregnant!" ("*selig aber ist der also Schwangere!*") (Z, 244; 4, 287). In the chorus, then,

> "Never yet did I find the woman by whom I wanted children, unless it be this woman, whom I love, for I love you, Oh Eternity!"

Here is a suggestion that the usual (Aristotelian) conception of generation is reversed. The singer is pregnant or longs for pregnancy but requires a woman for full procreation. This variation on pregnancy and birth will be echoed and varied once more (at least) in the story told in *Ecce Homo*, which could have been entitled "Why I Have Such Beautiful Children; or the Conception and Birth of My Son Zarathustra." Here all of the love and longing to give birth culminates in the sea bird. Let's read part of the final triad of "The Seven Seals":

> "If I love the sea and all that is sea-like, and love it most when it angrily contradicts me...
>
> If ever my rejoicing has cried: 'The shore has disappeared—now the last fetter falls from me...'
>
> And if it be my Alpha and Omega that everything heavy shall become light, every body a dancer, all spirit a bird (*aller Geist Vogel werde*): and truly that is my Alpha and Omega!...
>
> If ever I spread out a still sky above myself and flew with my own wings into my own sky:

If, playing, I have swum into deep light-distances *(Licht-Fernen)* and bird-wisdom came to my freedom:

But thus speaks bird-wisdom: 'Behold, there is no above, no below! Fling yourself about, out, back, you light one *(du Leichter)!* Sing! Speak no more!'" (Z, 246–247; 4, 290–291)

Spirit becomes bird. So that it will not stink, so that it need not feed on disgusting food; so that it can fly beyond the great nausea. Bird-wisdom is different from the teachings of spirit prior to its transformation. Spirit in its Germanic philosophical form teaches the lessons of time and history; it is very much a geopolitical teaching, a doctrine of the solid European land mass, not a teaching of sea and sky. Bird-wisdom, especially the wisdom of a bird who was born and gives birth without the security and fixity of the land, teaches that "there is no above, no below!" When spirit becomes bird there is a metamorphosis from the temporal-historical to the spatial-topological. Zarathustra could hardly be more emphatic in repeating that these three transformations:

> all that is heavy becomes light
> all body becomes dancer
> all spirit becomes bird

are his Alpha and Omega, the beginning and the end of his thought. Might not the first and last words of this wisdom have something to do with the process of birth? The bird is freed from the constraints of life on the land by its flight; the sea bird has even broader horizons.[31] Rilke, perhaps following a Nietzschean inspiration, speculated that various creatures live their relationships to their worlds in radically different ways, depending on the manner of their birth. Womb-born animals have a nostalgia for the interior (what Nietzsche appears to call *Geist* here) that can never be overcome. How could they ever fly with ease, as flight requires an unbounded play in space? "And how confused is anything that comes from a womb and has to fly. As if afraid of itself, it darts through the air like a crack through a cup, the way a wing of a bat crazes the porcelain of night."[32] Now the halcyon is doubly liberated from the land and its sedentary habits because it is a sea bird. But the halcyon also is hatched at sea, in a floating nest; it has never known the fixity of the nest on land and so will not be haunted by nostalgia for an immovable origin and will not be obsessed with restoring, recreating, and recapturing the origin. For such a creature words—discourse, sentences, lectures, essays, arguments—are too heavy; song is its mode of celebrating the light and boundless spaces where "there is no above, no below." Is such song the halcyon voice or tone that must be heard in *Zarathustra*?

Yet there is also the supplement, in many guises. Nietzsche acknowledges in *Ecce Homo* that there was postpartum distress: "There is something I call the *rancune* of what is great: everything great—a work, a deed—is no sooner accomplished than it turns *against* the man who did it. By doing it he has become *weak*" (EH, 303; 6, 342). But the text produces its own supplement, the posthalcyon composition of *Zarathustra* IV; no longer the beautiful melancholy cry of the sea bird nor her celebration of the boundless, but Zarathustra's temptation and the long, grating wail of a collective call of distress. The halcyon days are followed by the storms of winter.

Ecce Homo seeks to forge an identity between Nietzsche (who hatched the eggs), his halcyon son, Zarathustra, and his own current condition, another pregnancy as he prepares to "confront humanity with the most difficult demand ever made of it" (*EH*, 217; 6, 257). But in sending out this premature notice, an announcement of pregnancy rather than of birth, Nietzsche goes through what we might now call a hysterical pregnancy. He insists not only on the halcyon tone of *Zarathustra* but on his own ripeness, his own perfect weather. He offers us a retrospect and a prospect; for example in the interleaf passage that expresses a halcyon mood, the rich fall afternoon of a happy man:

> On this perfect day, when everything is ripening and not only the grape turns brown, the eye of the sun just fell upon my life: I looked back, I looked forward and never saw so many good things at once. It was not for nothing that I buried my forty-fourth year today; I had the right to bury it; whatever was life in it has been saved, is immortal. (*EH*, 221; 6, 263)

In halcyonic terms this may sound like the calm before the storm, the storm that erupted in January 1889, two weeks after the winter solstice, after the eggs had hatched, after the storm and after the sea god had unleashed the winds he had held in check. Indeed, at the beginning of the winter solstice of that year (December 21, 1888), Nietzsche wrote to his mother "The sun and clear sky always return as masters again after a few days of fog."[33]

It's not surprising that the thinker of eternal recurrence at this time of retrospect and prospect should have a desire, as he says, to tell his life to himself and that cyclical patterns and myths should loom large in that story. In *Ecce Homo* Nietzsche describes "how one becomes what one is" and emphasizes that "in order to become what one is one must not have the faintest notion what one is." The sense of one's story emerges only in the process. What Nietzsche knows now is that he is a bundle of binary oppositions, a machine of sorts that oscillates between the poles of these various pairs in an uncanny but determined way. Beginning from his initial declaration that "the secret of my existence is that I am alive as my mother and dead as my father," the set of binaries expands and proliferates, coming to include (at least):affirmation and negation, health and illness, being a beginning and being a decadent, Dionysus and the crucified, good and bad food and climates, being Polish and being German.

In the desire to construct a narrative around these various polarities we may see an instance of a procedure that Claude Lévi-Strauss claims is typical of all mythical thinking. *La pensée sauvage*, or untamed thought, constantly is faced with reconciling such opposed or contradictory elements. The Oedipus story, for example, bears the burden of making plausible a world in which men are born from the earth and in which they also have a higher origin, a world where family ties are both overvalued (through incest, for example) and undervalued (as in parricide). In writing a story of oneself, of a single person, the need for myth may be increased by the fact that the polarities are predicated of a single individual.[34]

So Nietzsche knits together a number of stories about illness and convalescence, periodic crisis and recovery, halcyon days and storms, that give some definition to what he has become and continues becoming. Perhaps these stories are all variants of one another in different keys. In several places Nietzsche portrays his life, in something of a medical vein, as proceeding by six year intervals whose ends are marked by crises of health and feeling. In a letter to Franz Overbeck of February 1883, Nietzsche writes "My whole life has crumbled under my gaze: this whole eerie, deliberately secluded life, which takes a step every six years, and actually wants nothing but the taking of this step." Presumably the most recent step is that of the (final) composition of *Zarathustra* I in January 1883, a time that Nietzsche associates with changes in earth and the heavens: "I, with my physical style of thinking, now see myself as the victim of a terrestrial and climatic disturbance to which Europe is exposed."[35] Six years later it will be the halcyon days and their aftermath in Turin, January 1889. Then there is the story of Sanctus Januarius (San Gennaro), whose blood liquifies every January in Naples (it also liquifies in May, but Nietzsche omits this part of the legend). We might think of this as a Christian version of the halcyon days. It could be thought of as a screen story by means of which an Anti-Christian, not yet the Antichrist, could acknowledge the psychic tensions of the Christmas season by invoking a non-Christian narrative. Freud interpreted an acquaintance's (or his own) reference to Saint January (San Gennaro) in Naples as a reference to the periodicity of menstruation and anxieties about pregnancy; Nietzsche's watch on the calendar of his own pregnancies also focuses on January.[36]

All of these stories serve as a kind of pledge or promise that every joy and every sorrow is tightly tied to all of the other moments of his existence. In a passage that Colli and Montinari have now restored to the text of *Ecce Homo*, we can see why Nietzsche would find such stories attractive:

> If I were to seek the deepest contradiction to me, an incalculable commonness of instinct, I would always find my mother and sister,—to believe myself related to such *canaille* would be a blasphemy against my divinity. The treatment that I have experienced from the side of my mother and sister, up until this moment, fills me with an

unspeakable horror: here a perfect infernal machine (*Höl-lenmaschine*) is at work, with an unfailing certainty as to the moment in which I can be bloodily wounded—in my highest moments...then one lacks all the strength to pro-tect oneself against the poisonous worm.... The physiolog-ical contiguity makes possible such a *disharmonia praestablita*.... But I recognize that the deepest objection to "eternal recurrence," my own most abysmal thought, is always mother and sister. (6, 268)[37]

To be trapped in an infernal machine that involves a preestablished *dis*harmony is incompatible with the notion of one's life as a fully integrated organic unity. But it is not inconsis-tent with six year cycles, Sanctus Januarius, and the periodic return of the halcyon days. There is a thoroughgoing polemic in Nietzsche against modern, teleological, linear narrative, the kind of story that we have come to call Hegelian in which life, personal or social, is represented according to the grammar of the *Bildungsroman*. Nietzsche's stories may remind us rather of the more elemental process that Freud observed in his one-and-a-half-year-old grandson, who played the game of *fort!-da!*, making his toy periodically disappear and reappear. Freud spec-ulates that this is a symbolic way of dealing with the appearance and disappearance of the mother. And Jacques Lacan adds that as symbolic (linguistic) activity, it manages to avoid both the delusions of the imaginary, in which the child constructs an illu-sionary, hyperbolical image of his power and self-sufficiency, and the terrors of the real, in which he is subject to continued assaults, pains, and challenges. For Nietzsche the terms are reversed. The approach of mother and sister is dreaded; peaceful days consist in holding them at a distance. And as in a dream, the Alcyone story reverses a number of genders and relations. It is the divine father (Aeolus) who protects the breeding female, rather than the mother who endangers the male. Nietzsche liked to think of himself as pregnant, as hatching eggs. To have a sense for the halcyon is to know that such eggs are protected. So Aris-totle's long and fascinated description of the floating halcyon nest attempted to give a realistic account of the materials that went into the construction of such a miracle of engineering.[38]

This protection and self-sufficiency is counterposed to many storms. For example, to the confusions of the historical sense as Nietzsche writes in *Beyond Good and Evil:*

> Let us finally own it to ourselves: what we men of the "historical sense" find most difficult to grasp, to feel, to taste once more, to love once more, what at bottom finds us prejudiced and almost hostile, is precisely the perfection and ultimate maturity of every culture and art, that which is really noble in a work or human being, the moment when their sea is smooth and they have found halcyon self-sufficiency, the golden and cold aspect of all things that have consummated themselves. (*BGE*, 224; 5, 159)

With all our historical sense what "we" find most difficult to grasp is *halkyonischer Selbstgenugsamkeit.* This section follows immediately on the one in which Nietzsche suggests that in the world of the "hybrid European" who is in desperate need of a constant change of costumes we may turn this apparent lack of identity into a virtue by donning the costumes for "a carnival in the grand style" and becoming "parodists of world's history and God's buffoons (*Hanswürste*)." That is, it contrasts the halcyon and the parasitic. And of course we are just now exercising our historical sense and our historical activity by remembering that Nietzsche was a classicist who knew his stories and knew how they could be lost or distorted. We find it difficult not to play the philologist with Nietzsche's text, turning everything into fragments and alternative versions. Let's remember, thinking of Lévi-Strauss's work, that there is no unique or authentic version of any myth. All that we have to do to confirm this is to consult the *Pauly-Wissowa Real-encyclopadie der classischen Altertumswissenschaft,* and we discover that already in antiquity is a form of the legend according to which Alcyone and Keyx got what they deserved. It probably started with Hesiod, who is already a somewhat dialectical thinker, a thinker of history and becoming, for whom time is infected with transgression and retribution until redeemed by the rigor of the Olympians. Hesiod's lost work *Keyx gamos (Keyx's wedding)* is most likely the source of the story preserved by Apollodorus, who says: "These perished by reason of their pride; for he said that his wife was Hera, and she said that her husband was Zeus. But Zeus turned them into birds; her he made a halcyon and him a ceyx (gannet)."[39]

Of course there is a related story even in Ovid, who seems to present Alcyone and Keyx as flawless. Why did Keyx undertake that voyage anyway, even though Alcyone pleaded with him so lovingly and so desperately not to go? He'd been distracted by a series of horrors, the first of which was his brother's transformation into a ferocious bird of prey (the evil relative of the halcyon?); that was occasioned by his daughter's boasting that she was more beautiful than Diana, after two gods had mounted her in one day. Why do we learn this from Ovid at the point where Keyx is introduced? Ovid tells the story in the way that it's become most popular, but there's a trace of the other one. Not for Friedrich Nietzsche, though. No spot seems to touch the halcyon he knows, the one under attack from the historical sense, the one that gives its rare tone to Zarathustra. No, the innocence of becoming requires that we think of the halcyon as blameless, as innocent. It apparently is in such a mood that Nietzsche inscribes the halcyon in the retrospect of *Thus Spoke Zarathustra* that constitutes the prospect (that is, the *Vorrede*) of *Toward a Genealogy of Morals*. This is then a forereading, a protocol that looks forward to the reading of the *Genealogy.* Someone might have trouble reading the *Genealogy,* says Nietzsche:

> If this book is incomprehensible to anyone and jars on his ears, the fault, it seems to me is not necessarily mine. It is clear enough, assuming, as I do assume, that one has first read my earlier writings and has not spared some trouble in doing so: for they are, indeed, not easy to penetrate. Regarding my *Zarathustra,* for example, I do not allow that anyone knows that book who has not at some time been profoundly wounded and at some time profoundly delighted by every word in it; for only then may he enjoy the privilege of reverentially sharing in the halcyon element out of which that book was born and in its sunlight clarity, remoteness, breadth and certainty. (*GM,* 22; 5, 255)

The reading that must precede the reading of both the *Genealogy* and *Ecce Homo* is *Zarathustra*. But we're already talking of faults here; of the reader who has one, or one of the others, one of the halcyon ones, who knows he's avoided a fault. Ovid's Alcyone, we suppose, knew that she had avoided going the way of Keyx's niece and insulting the gods. Readers, you must painfully work up to the halcyon; you'll be wounded and delighted. The *Geneal-ogy* itself will be part of the work of getting to the "halcyon ele-ment"; in fact its last essay, as Nietzsche says, is an example of the *Auslegung* of a single aphorism from *Zarathustra*. Is this a hermeneutic circle or a halcyonic cycle? The circle does not nec-essarily involve being both profoundly wounded and delighted by every word or every aphorism in it. The circle moves in the direction of a fusion of horizons. The cycle is varied, cosmic, it provides a sense of "clarity, remoteness, breadth, and certainty": infinite horizons. It will be a long time, Nietzsche says, before his writings are "readable." in *Ecce Homo* he'll add that we won't understand *Zarathustra* unless we *hear* its halcyon tone. If we don't hear it, we'll be committing a "wretched injustice." Neither readable nor hearable without the halcyon. The aphorism set for *Auslegung*, it seems, has to do with woman's love, wisdom, and the warrior; that is, it has to do with sexual difference, our knowledge of that difference, and the way in which such knowl-edge is involved in reading and writing: "Unconcerned, mock-ing, violent—thus wisdom wants *us*: she is a woman and always loves only a warrior." Maybe we'll come to see what that apho-rism means. Is wisdom bird wisdom? Perhaps the aphorism describes Alcyone's lover: the halcyon element would be here. Where? In an essay about the meaning of ascetic ideals that enacts the self-criticism of science and its transvaluation. It is a "twisting free" of science, if art is not simply thought according to the metaphysics of presence. Or is the aphorism one more pro-tocol of reading? After all, it comes from the chapter "*Vom Lesen und Schreiben*." Can we read in a way that Alcyone might love?

Can we find Alcyone in *Thus Spoke Zarathustra*? Is it her voice that whispers the "Midnight Song"? Will we find her as a woman or a bird, "fluttering her broken wings" ("On the After-worldly") or swimming "playfully in the deep light-distances" enjoying the "bird wisdom of [her] freedom" ("The Seven

Seals")? In the last of "The Seven Seals" Zarathustra proposes marriage to eternity with the nuptial ring of rings while letting bird wisdom *speak:* "'bird-wisdom speaks thus: 'Behold, there is no above, no below! Fling yourself about, out, back, you who are light! Sing! Speak no more! Are not all words made for the grave and heavy?'" (Z, 247; 4, 291). Is this the answer of the woman Zarathustra would espouse or is it the halcyon tone that comes from the mouth of the book?

In the retrospective accounts of *Zarathustra* that serve as prospects for his later writings, both published and planned, the halcyon function comes to involve the reader as well. For the voice to speak or sing we must listen and read. If the halcyon is the most difficult both to hear and understand, as Nietzsche says in *Beyond Good and Evil*, it is also presupposed insofar as one has good taste in reading or music, that is, in listening. So we should listen attentively when Nietzsche speaks of *"we halcyons,"* underlining the phrase, in *The Case of Wagner*, where he listens forward and backward to the career of music and the Germans to explain what listening is. After noting deep affinities between the German taste for Hegel and the German taste for Wagner, Nietzsche suggests that such minds must be situated, first of all, by means of their meteorological attunements:

> Trembling, they hear how the *great symbols* approach from foggy distances to resound in [Wagner's] art with muted thunder; they are not impatient when at times things are gray, gruesome and cold. After all, they are, without exception, like Wagner himself, *related* to such bad weather, German weather! Wotan is their god; but Wotan is the god of bad weather.
>
> They are quite right, these German youths, considering what they are like: how could they miss what we others, *we halcyons* [*wir Halkyonier* Nietzsche's emphasis] miss in Wagner—*la gaya scienza*; light feet, wit, fire, grace; the great logic; the exuberant spirituality; the southern shivers of light; the *smooth (glatte)* sea-perfection... (CW, 10; 6, 37)

Here Nietzsche introduces *halcyon* into the German language and German musicology; or we might say that he would like to seduce the Germans by means of the halcyon. In any case the contrast between the German (in its usual form) and the halcyon is drawn sharply. Who are *we* halcyons? Let's recall that there are two traditions about Alcyone and Keyx. In one they are both turned into halcyons or kingfishers; in another they are separated into two different species, Alcyone as a halcyon and Keyx as an ornithologically unidentifiable bird that bears his name. *We halcyons* may be one gender or two, but we will not be exclusively male.

According to Heidegger, Nietzsche stands at the end of Western metaphysics, having achieved a complete inversion of its essential principles. But Nietzsche himself tells us that we cannot understand him or his texts if we do not hear the halcyon tone that speaks or cries through them. As a cry this tone also echoes through the Western tradition, if not so obviously through its metaphysical core; we might remember, for example, that the first sinners Dante encounters in hell are Paolo and Francesca, two lovers given the eternal form of birds. The earliest documented appearance of the halcyon's cry is in Book Nine of the *Iliad*, and it appears in a way that can be articulated with the fate of the metaphysical tradition. In Homer, Alcyone is mentioned in the course of the embassy to Achilles, as part of a story that Phoinix tells to Achilles about Meleager, another hero who withdrew from battle in anger. Meleager rejects his battle duties and lies apart with his wife, Kleopatra, whose own genealogy as the daughter of Idas and Marpessa is given in what the critics call a digression. Then there is this passage: "A girl, her father and honoured mother had named in their palace Alcyone, sea-bird, as a by-name, since for her sake her mother with the sorrow-laden cry of a sea-bird wept because far- reaching Phoibos Apollo had taken her."[40] The undecidability of pronominal reference in the Greek text is like that observed in this English translation by Richmond Lattimore. It could be either Marpessa or her daughter, Kleopatra, who was nicknamed *Alcyone*. It makes a difference, for here Alcyone is said to be named after the bird because in some way she shared or imitated the bird's fate and its cry. The reading found most plausible has been that Kleopatra was called Alcyone on account of the sorrow of Marpessa, her mother, who was seized by Apollo from her husband Idas.[41] The commentators point out that the whole story of Idas, Marpessa and Kleopatra/Alkyone has the tone of an older story, perhaps another epic fragment, that was incorporated into Homer.[42] Someone was crying and lamenting; it was a woman, but we're not completely sure who she was or why she cried. Is the cry a cry of revenge, the revenge against time and its "it was"? In notes of 1882–1883, Nietzsche says "It's impossible to suffer without wanting someone to pay for it; already every complaint or lament contains revenge (*schon jede Klage enthält Rache*)" (*10, 190*). (These notes echo some of Emerson's essays.) Is the halcyon tone always already laced with revenge? The context of the story could suggest that, since Phoinix is part of the embassy to Achilles and he tells him a story of how *not* to act, that is, *not* like Meleager, whose life was infected by revenge, whose wife's genealogy involved parents who complained against the gods and named their children so as to give that complaint a living embodiment. In Homer's version then, the first that we know of, although it seems to refer back to a lost story, Alcyone is a secondary name; the woman is named after the bird, not the bird after the woman. The sorrowful song is passed on from parents to children; perhaps, there was no Alcyone before the sorrows. Our parents sang the blues, and we find ourselves singing them too. They chose our names so we wouldn't forget that old song. Here in Apollonian Homer, it's a bit of tragic Dionysian wisdom and music.

This, however, was not the lesson that Phoinix set out to teach with his story, even though he too is a man of sorrows. He was driven from home after sleeping with his father's mistress at his mother's instigation. His father laid the curse of childlessness on him. And now he pleads with Achilles, his substitute son, to accept the gifts of Agamemnon and rejoin the Greeks. The whole point of the story of Meleager is that he too was offered gifts to lay his anger aside and return to battle; although he spurned those gifts at first, he eventually relented and fought on the side of his people. But by then it was too late to get the gifts; the offer no longer was valid. The commentators point out that Homer apparently has altered the Meleager story to make it serve as an example or model in which almost all the aspects of the story parallel those of Achilles' situation.[43] So Phoinix is saying, don't suffer the fate of Meleager and Kleopatra, of Alkyone and the bird she's named after; it is not impossible, all you have to do is reenter the economy of gifts that Agamemnon temporarily disrupted when he seized your beautiful girl-prize, Briseis: "No, with gifts promised go forth. The Achaians will honour you as they would an immortal. But if without gifts you go into the fighting where men perish, your honour will no longer be as great, though you drive back the battle." Achilles' answer is crucial and famous: "Such honour is a thing I need not. I think I am honored already in Zeus's ordinance..."

So honor is not a question of the circulation of gifts, of the delicacies of diplomatic exchange (like the great exchange of armor by Glaukos and Diomedes in Book VI), nor of the ceremonial reception of guests and the giving of feasts and potlatches and burning great sides of beef for the gods. It denotes an intrinsic relation to a higher principle, to Zeus, as if Zeus himself were not caught up in such an economy. Phoinix represents the old wisdom; Achilles the new. And as Achilles rejects Phoinix's advice, he also, at the same time, and with the same gesture dismisses all of this talk about cries, complaints, and distress: "Stop confusing my heart with lamentation and sorrow for the favour of great Atreides." The lamentations that Achilles rejects here are a woman's tears, wails, and sorrows. Socrates will echo this rejection later in the *Republic* when it is said that lamentations are not for men, that even a good woman ought not to be allowed the harmonies appropriate to sorrow, and that a man ought not to be shown imitating a woman "who's caught in the grip of misfortune, mourning and wailing. And we'll be far from needing one [a woman] who's sick or in love or in labor" (*Republic* 387c, 395d, 398c).

Perhaps this site is as plausible a candidate as any for the "beginning" of Western metaphysics. Achilles is rejecting the gift economy, in which honor circulates and is at the mercy of arbitrary events and capricious figures like Agamemnon; in that world honor can be given and taken away with equal ease. These presents are not truly or genuinely present; they are hostages to fortune. There is a more genuine honor, honor from Zeus, whose presence cannot be shaken by men or death. The entire Olympian order is not invoked here, for those quarreling gods reproduce the ambiguities of the human world of exchange. Zeus alone is named, for he presides over a world in which a single standard of truth is obtainable. Nietzsche had suggested in *The Genealogy of Morals* that the deepest opposition was not among competing philosophical conceptions of truth, but between art and science: "Plato versus Homer: there is the complete, the genuine antagonism—there the sincerest advocate of the 'beyond,' the great slanderer of life; here the instinctive deifier, the *golden* nature" (*GM*, III, 25; 5, 402–403). But just as Heidegger had to recognize a sense of truth as correctness rather than as dis-closure (*aletheia*) even in Homer, so Nietzsche might have to acknowledge that the opposition of Plato and Homer is to be found in Homer himself.[44] For Achilles, in rejecting gifts and noisy women's lamentations for the sake of an eternal honor, an honor grounded in the beyond, is the precursor of Socrates and Plato. When Socrates cites Achilles in the *Apology*, he is articulating this "original" metaphysics in which genuine and fake honor are juxtaposed.[45] The sense of truth as correctness, as a present adequation whose own presence need not be explained, is a sense that (as Heidegger would remind us) fails to hear the giving in *es gibt*. At this crisis in the history of ethics and metaphysics, Homer has inscribed a number of fateful names in the story of Meleager, names that summon up thoughts of love, devotion, and lamentation, that just might limit or deform the metaphysics that is instituting itself, but that remain as traces, in the guise of what we call myths. It was Kleopatra, the devoted wife, who pled with Meleager. This name, Kleopatra, the scholars have not failed to note, corresponds by a reversal of syllables to that of Patroclus, Achilles' own beloved.[46] Phoinix could be suggesting that Achilles' Patroclus would want to plead with him as Kleopatra did with Meleager. But in constructing his example, with all of its implicit and explicit parallelisms Phoinix has already begun to speak that discourse of a universalistic ethics which Achilles will push several stages further and on whose precedent Socrates will want to rely. For if indeed there are such general principles for human conduct that apply to both a Meleager and an Achilles, the lovers of Kleopatra/Alkyone and Patroclus, then are we not committed (this is Achilles' question) to finding the most universal and comprehensively grounded of these (those sanctioned by Zeus) and ignoring all other considerations? So Achilles doesn't need to *listen* to those who have come to entreat him—not to Phoinix or even to Patroclus, should he choose to echo the thoughts of the elders. "Don't bother me with lamentations," Achilles says, dismissing and disclaiming a certain halcyon tone. Alkyone is another name for Kleopatra; because the latter was probably invented for the occasion, it's perhaps a way of indicating that the sorrowing voice that holds out for the life of a loving companion, in the last analysis, is not a strict proper name, if there is such a thing. And should there be something to Heidegger's conception of Nietzsche as the last metaphysician, then it may be important to hear this tone that seems to cry out both at the beginning and end of the metaphysical tradition. When the embassy to Achilles seeks to bring him back into the battle the speakers pull out all the rhetorical weapons of a warrior society; Book Nine of the *Iliad* often is cited as the earliest paradigm of Greek rhetoric. The last and most moving of these pleas, the one that represents the most archaic level of the appeal, is the one in which a very old man, at an exceptional moment, seeks to bring a woman's voice into the conversation. It is this voice with its tone of lamentation and its history of sorrows that Achilles rejects. He will be more of a man, he insists, than these three great men who have come to him.

Now we may seem to be very distant from Nietzsche who celebrated Homer and his heroes in contrast to Socrates and science. But when Nietzsche tells us in the strongest terms that we fail to understand him unless we hear his halcyon tone, is there a trace or memory of this cry that echoes at one of the earliest sites of Western metaphysics and its ethos? It may be a tone, a voice, and a cry that Nietzsche, the celebrant of the ancient idea of inspiration, did not completely control. It speaks of gifts, friends, lovers, and pregnancy rather than of eternal meanings and values. It does not lament so much for the loss of an archaic world as it sings of open skies and infinite watery horizons. It speaks of metamorphosis rather than honor from Zeus.

Notes

1. Cf. *Deutsches Fremdwörterbuch*, ed. Hans Schulz (Strassburg 1913; reprinted Berlin, 1974), pp. 261–262. Today the word has commercial uses (at least in English); there is a prescription sleeping pill called *Halcion* and a bed and breakfast establishment with the name *Halcyon House* in Lawrence, Kansas. Both uses suggest the sense of "sublime peace" (*erhabene Ruhe*) cited in the *Deutsches Fremdwörterbuch*. The Halcion pill, however, has recently been discovered to have the undecidable qualities of a *pharmakon*—drug, poison, dose, remedy—as it has been suspected of causing memory loss as well as being an effective sleeping potion.

2. The stories of Alcyone and references to the ancient literature are recapitulated most conveniently in the article "Alcyone" in the *Pauly-Wissowa Realenzklopädie der classischen Altertumswissenschaft* (Stuttgart, 1984), vol. 1, columns 1579–1581.

See also D'Arcy Thompson, *A Glossary of Greek Birds*, 2d ed. (Oxford, 1936), pp. 46–51; and Norman Douglas, *Birds and Beasts of the Greek Anthology* (New York, 1929), pp. 111–118. A more recent scholarly treatment is found in Gerald K. Gresseth "The Myth of Alcyone" in *Transactions and Proceedings of the American Philological Association*, 95 (1964): 88–98.

3. Ernst Bertram, *Nietzsche: Versuch einer Mythologie* (Berlin, 1921). Bertram's chapter "Claude Lorrain" (pp. 249–260) traces some of Nietzsche's articulations of the opposition between north and south and his evocations of ideal landscape and climate that are relevant to the halcyon theme. C. G. Jung's works abound in discussion of Nietzsche and myth, but now see in particular his published seminar *Nietzsche's Zarathustra*, 2 vols., ed. James L. Jarrett (Princeton, N.J., 1988). These lengthy volumes contain a wealth of speculations and associations by Jung and his seminarists as they slowly work through the text of *Zarathustra* (their work was interrupted by World War II and never resumed). They are rewarding if read with some caution. Hans Blumenberg's *Work on Myth* presents a novel and provocative view of the continual reworking, rewriting and commentary on myths in the European tradition as in solidarity with the Enlightenment project of mastering the unknown; his discussion of Nietzsche focuses on the latter's variations on the Prometheus myth; see Blumenberg, *Work on Myth*, trans. Robert M. Wallace (Cambridge, Mass., 1985), pp. 604–622.

4. Ovid, *Metamorphoses* XI, lines 725–748; the translation is by Horace Gregory (New York, 1958).

5. See Michel Foucault, *The Care of the Self* (*The History of Sexuality*, vol. 3), trans. Robert Hurley (New York, 1986). Given Foucault's project of analyzing the discourses of sexuality insofar as they attempt to assess the best way of handling erotic matters in a wide variety of social, political, and medical contexts, it is understandable that he would not consider the more "figurative" or "literary" expressions of eros during the same period. It is notable, however, that some of the writers Foucault examines (most notably Plutarch) parallel their medical or philosophical discussion of love affairs with myths like that of the halcyon that provide cosmic parallels for their books of practical advice. Elsewhere I have expressed my hesitations about Foucault's narrowed and reductive account of some of the classical texts; see my "Translating, Repeating, Naming: Foucault, Derrida and the Genealogy of Morals" in *Nietzsche as Postmodernist*, ed. Clayton Koelb (Albany, 1990), pp. 39–55.

6. *Pauly-Wissowa*, column 1581.

7. Aristotle, *History of Animals*, 542 b 24.

8. Ibid., 542b7–11.

9. Ibid., 542b2–3

10. Ibid., 616a15–32.

11. Thompson, *A Glossary of Greek Birds*, 1 ed. (Oxford, 1896), p. 29. 12. *History of Animals*, 487a20–21.

13. See, for example, the note by T. E. Page to Virgil, *Georgics* I, line 399, in Virgil, *Bucolies and Georgics* (London, 1931), pp. 230–231.

14. For the view of the *History of Animals* as "a public notebook in which new facts were recorded as they cam to hand," see D. J. Allan, *The Philosophy of Aristotle*, (Oxford, 1970), p. 67.

15. Plutarch, "On the Cleverness of Animals," *Moralia*, 982–983.

16. D'Arcy Thompson, note to his translation of Aristotle, *History of Animals* (Oxford, 1910), 616a.

17. Emerson, *Lectures and Essays* (New York, 1983), p. 541.

18. Thompson, *A Glossary of Greed Birds*, 2 ed., pp. 49–50.

19. Gresseth, "The Myth of Alcyone," p. 93.

20. Norman Douglas, *Birds and Beasts of the Greek Anthology*, pp. 113–114.

21. Lucian, *Selections from Lucian*, trans. Emily James Smith (New York, 1892), p. 283; see also the German translation of the same dialogue "*Der Eisvogel oder die Verwandlung*," in Lukian, *Sämtliche Werke*, trans. Wieland and Floerke, (Berlin, 1922), Bd. 5, pp. 1–7, with useful notes.

22. Ovid, *Metamorphoses* XI, lines 85-220.

23. Sander Gilman, *Conversations with Nietzsche*, trans. David J. Parent (New York, 1987), pp. 155–157.

24. Ibid., p. 159.

25. Alcman (no. 26) in *Lyra Graeca*, vol. 1, ed. and trans. J. M. Edmonds (New York, 1922), p. 73.

26. This sketch, in particular the conjunction of the halcyon and the theme of Caesar among the pirates has a curious parallel in Shakespeare's *Henry VI: I*. Henry's enemy, Joan of Arc (Joan La Pucelle), says this of herself as she plans to do battle:

> Asign'd am I to be the English scourge.
> This night the siege assuredly I'll raise:
> Expect Saint Martin's summer, halcyon days,
> Since I have entered into these wars.
> Glory is like a circle in the water,
> Which never ceaseth to enlarge itself
> Till by broad spreading it disperse to nought.
> With Henry's death the English circle ends:
> Dispersed are the flories it included.
> Now am I like that proud insulting ship
> Which Caesar and his fortune bare at once.
> (I. ii. 129–139)

To associate the halcyon days with Joan of Arc involves a complex gesture regarding gender, for she is traditionally a woman who plays the role of a man. However, there is irony in her reference to the "proud insulting ship," for she, like the pirates, eventually will be defeated. Shakespeare's other reference to the halcyon, in *King Lear*, also has a negative tone; there Kent condemns those "rogues" who

> Renege, affirm, and turn their halcyon beaks
> With every gale and vary of their masters
> (II. ii. 84–85)

This is a reference to the belief that a dead and dried halcyon hung up somewhere, as on a ship's mast, could foretell the weather by the direction in which it pointed.

27. Although Nietzsche never used these titles for a published work, others (whom I now join) have composed "halcyons." Gabriele D'Annunzio's collection of poems *Alcyone*, which appeared in 1903, may well be indebted to Nietzsche. A number of the poems are called dithyrambs and women, the sea, and the classical world are celebrated throughout. The settings are summery, however, rather than at the winter solstice. Vera Brittain's 1929 book *Halcyon, or the Future of Monogamy* begins with a brief account of the myth of the text. Brittain's work is a tongue-in cheek transcription of a dream in which the author read a text reporting the fate of sexuality 100 years in the future. The halcyon here carries the Hellenistic sense of devoted married love. The imaginary history is a somewhat Hegelian progression in which the major epochs are the unreasonable repression of the Victorians, the frantic license of the early and middle twentieth century, concluding with the happy and faithful monogamy of the time of the author of the report (our and Brittain's future).

28. Cf. Thompson, *A Glossary of Greek Birds*, 2d ed., pp. 49–51; and Gresseth, "The Myth of Alcyone," p. 93.

29. To Carl Fuchs, Nietzsche wrote *"Die fröhliche Wissenschaft,* 'la gaya sceinza,' you certainly must read: it is my most medial book—a great deal of subtle joy, a great deal of halcyonism" (letter of July 29, 1888: *Briefe* 8, 376; Middleton, *Selected Letters*, p. 305).

30. Cf. Jacques Derrida, *Of Spirit*, trans. Geoffrey Bennington and Rachel Bowlby (Chicago, 1989).

31. Gaston Bachelard in his chapter "Nietzsche and the Ascensional Psyche" in *Air and Dreams* describes the intensity of Nietzsche's aerial imagination in such texts as these, and devotes some attention to Nietzsche's/Zarathustra's fantasies of being a bird. His commentary, however, is restricted by his conception of the "material imagination" which he takes to be responsible for these motifs. Such an approach tends to look at Nietzsche as simply working out the consequences of a spontaneous and originary character; a more linguistically and textually oriented reading would notice, for example, that when Zarathustra speaks of the wonders of fresh air it is in contrast to air polluted by parasites and that the particular sort of aerial calm he values is inscribed with the halcyon and the name (Alcyone) from

which it is derived; Bachelard falls too easily into a method of elimination, according to which Nietzsche is not a poet of earth, fire, or water and so must have an aerial imagination—this of course neglects the halcyon conjunction of water and air. See *Air and Dreams*, trans. Edith R. Farrell and C. Frederick Farrell (Dallas, 1988), esp. pp. 138–139, 142–143, 146, 152–155.

32. Rainer Maria Rilke, *Duino Elegies* 8, trans. A. Poulin (Boston, 1977). See also the notes to this elegy in the translation by J. B. Leishman and Stephen Spender (New York, 1963), pp. 108–111.

33. *Briefe*, 8, p. 542; in Middleton, *Selected Letters of Friedrich Nietzsche*, p. 336.

34. Cf. *Nietzschean Narratives*, pp. 160–161.

35. Nietzsche to Franz Overbeck, February 10, 1883; *Briefe* vol. 6, pp. 325–326; trans. Christopher Middleton, *Selected Letters of Friedrich Nietzsche* (Chicago, 1969), pp. 206–207.

36. For Freud's account, see *The Psychopathology of Everyday Life*, trans. A. A. Brill in *The Basic Writings of Sigmund Freud* (New York, 1938), pp. 41–45.

37. Trans. Tracy Strong in Daniel O'Hara, ed. *Why Nietzsche Now?* (Bloomington, 1985), p. 327.

38. Aristotle, *History of Animals*, 616a15–34.

39. Appolodorus, *The Library* I.VII.4, trans. Sir James George Frazer (Cambridge, Mass. , 1921).

40. Homer, *Iliad* IX, lines 561–564, trans. Richmond Lattimore (Chicago, 1963).

41. This is the view taken in the Pauly-Wissowa article "Alkyone": "That the name Alkyone was already at an early time tied to the concept of faithful married love and to a loving lament is shown by *Iliad* IX 562, where it is employed in this way as the nickname (*Beiname*) of Kleopatra, the wife of Meleager" (column 1587).

42. Cf. Walter Leaf, ed. , *The Iliad* (London, 1900), p. 413 n.; and M. M. Willcock, *The Iliad of Homer* (London, 1978), p. 282.

43. For a full account of the Meleager story, its artful parallels to Achilles' situation, and its variants in other texts, see Johannes Kakridis, *Homeric Researches* (Lund, 1949), pp. 11–42.

44. See Paul Friedlander, *Plato: An Introduction*, trans. Hans Meyerhoff (New York, 1964), pp. 221–229.

45. Plato, *Apology* 28b–c.

46. See Kakridis, *Homeric Researches*, p. 28, and the references given there.

INDEX